T0373823

AMERICAN EMPOWER

STUDENT'S BOOK A

WITH DIGITAL PACK

A1

STARTER

Adrian Doff, Craig Thaine
Herbert Puchta, Jeff Stranks, Peter Lewis-Jones
with Rachel Godfrey

CAMBRIDGE

AMERICAN EMPOWER is a six-level general English course for adult and young adult learners, taking students from beginner to advanced level (CEFR A1 to C1). *American Empower* combines course content from Cambridge University Press with validated assessment from the experts at Cambridge Assessment English.

American Empower's unique mix of engaging classroom materials and reliable assessment enables learners to make consistent and measurable progress.

Content you'll love.
Assessment you
can trust.

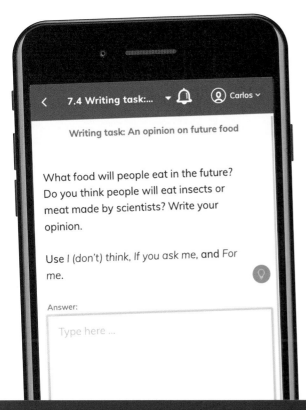

Better Learning with *American Empower*

Better Learning is our simple approach where **insights** we've gained from research have helped shape **content** that drives **results**.

Learner engagement

1 Content that informs and motivates

Insights
Sustained motivation is key to successful language learning and skills development.

Content
Clear learning goals, thought-provoking images, texts, and speaking activities, plus video content to arouse curiosity.

Results
Content that surprises, entertains, and provokes an emotional response, helping teachers to deliver motivating and memorable lessons.

2 Personalized and relevant

Insights
Language learners benefit from frequent opportunities to personalize their responses.

Content
Personalization tasks in every unit make the target language more meaningful to the individual learner.

Results
Personal responses make learning more memorable and inclusive, with all students participating in spontaneous spoken interaction.

> **❝** *There are so many adjectives to describe such a wonderful series, but in my opinion it's very reliable, practical, and modern.* **❞**
>
> **Zenaide Brianez, Director of Studies, Instituto da Língua Inglesa, Brazil**

Measurable progress

1 Assessment you can trust

Insights
Tests developed and validated by Cambridge Assessment English, the world leaders in language assessment, to ensure they are accurate and meaningful.

Content
End-of-unit tests, mid- and end-of-course competency tests, and personalized CEFR test report forms provide reliable information on progress with language skills.

Results
Teachers can see learners' progress at a glance, and learners can see measurable progress, which leads to greater motivation.

Results of an impact study showing % improvement of Reading levels, based on global *Empower* students' scores over one year.

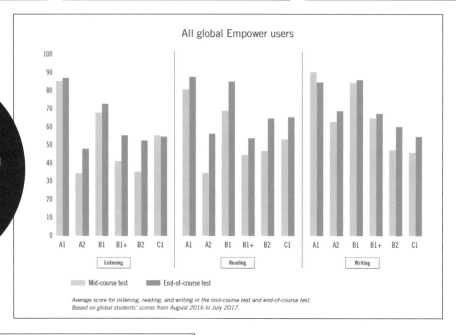

All global Empower users

Mid-course test   End-of-course test

Average score for listening, reading, and writing in the mid-course test and end-of-course test. Based on global students' scores from August 2016 to July 2017.

Cambridge English Empower B1+ intermediate
Competency test
Estimated CEFR level

Student Name:
Report Date:

You are now at the level to prepare for Cambridge English: PET

Skill
End of course level indicator

Overall
Reading
Listening
Writing
Speaking

Close to B1   B1 level   Good performance   Strong performance
Competency

Please note:
The Mid-course level indicator is replaced by the End-of-course level indicator.
The Reading, Listening and Writing sections are automatically scored. The score for the Speaking section is entered by your teacher.

CAMBRIDGE
UNIVERSITY PRESS

Cambridge Assessment
English

> *We started using the tests provided with Empower and our students started showing better results from this point until now.*

Kristina Ivanova, Director of Foreign Language Training Centre, ITMO University, Saint Petersburg, Russia

2 Evidence of impact

Insights
Schools and colleges need to show that they are evaluating the effectiveness of their language programs.

Content
Empower (British English) impact studies have been carried out in various countries, including Russia, Brazil, Turkey, and the UK, to provide evidence of positive impact and progress.

Results
Colleges and universities have demonstrated a significant improvement in language level between the mid- and end-of-course tests, as well as a high level of teacher satisfaction with *Empower*.

Manageable learning

1 Mobile friendly

Insights
Learners expect online content to be mobile friendly but also flexible and easy to use on any digital device.

Content
American Empower provides easy access to Digital Workbook content that works on any device and includes practice activities with audio.

Results
Digital Workbook content is easy to access anywhere, and produces meaningful and actionable data so teachers can track their students' progress and adapt their lesson accordingly.

> *I had been studying English for 10 years before university, and I didn't succeed. But now with Empower I know my level of English has changed.*

Nikita, *Empower* Student, ITMO University, Saint Petersburg, Russia

2 Corpus-informed

Insights
Corpora can provide valuable information about the language items learners are able to learn successfully at each CEFR level.

Content
Two powerful resources – Cambridge Corpus and English Profile – informed the development of the *Empower* course syllabus and the writing of the materials.

Results
Learners are presented with the target language they are able to incorporate and use at the right point in their learning journey. They are not overwhelmed with unrealistic learning expectations.

Rich in practice

1 Language in use

Insights
It is essential that learners are offered frequent and manageable opportunities to practice the language they have been focusing on.

Content
Throughout the *American Empower* Student's Book, learners are offered a wide variety of practice activities, plenty of controlled practice, and frequent opportunities for communicative spoken practice.

Results
Meaningful practice makes new language more memorable and leads to more efficient progress in language acquisition.

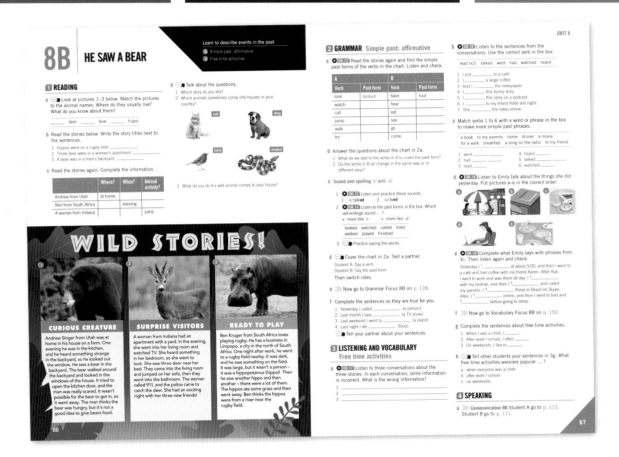

2 Beyond the classroom

There are plenty of opportunities for personalization.

Elena Pro, Teacher, EOI de San Fernando de Henares, Spain

Insights
Progress with language learning often requires work outside of the classroom, and different teaching models require different approaches.

Content
American Empower is available with a print workbook, online practice, documentary-style videos that expose learners to real-world English, plus additional resources with extra ideas and fun activities.

Results
This choice of additional resources helps teachers to find the most effective ways to motivate their students both inside and outside the classroom.

Unit overview

Unit Opener

Getting started page – Clear learning objectives to give an immediate sense of purpose.

▼

Lessons A and B

Grammar and Vocabulary – Input and practice of core grammar and vocabulary, plus a mix of skills.

Digital Workbook (online, mobile): Grammar and Vocabulary.

▼

Lesson C

Everyday English – Functional language in common, everyday situations.

Digital Workbook (online, mobile): Listening, Speaking, Reading, and Writing

▼

Unit Progress Test

▼

Review

Extra practice of grammar, vocabulary, and pronunciation. Also a "Review your progress" section for students to reflect on the unit.

▼

Mid- / End-of-course test

▼

Additional practice

Further practice is available for outside of the class with these components.

Digital Workbook (online, mobile)

Workbook (printed)

Components

Resources – Available on cambridgeone.org

- Audio
- Video
- Unit Progress Tests (Print)
- Unit Progress Tests (Online)

- Mid- and end-of-course assessment (Print)
- Mid- and end-of-course assessment (Online)

- Digital Workbook (Online)
- Photocopiable Grammar, Vocabulary, and Pronunciation worksheets

CONTENTS

Lesson and objective		Grammar	Vocabulary	Pronunciation	Everyday English
Unit 1 Hello!					
Getting started Talk about countries and flags					
1A	Say your name and country	*be*: *I* / *you* / *we*	Countries	Sound and spelling: *I'm, we're*	
1B	Talk about people you know	*be*: *he* / *she* / *they*	Nationalities; *this* / *these*	Syllables and word stress	
1C	Meet and greet new people			Syllables and word stress; Stressed words; Intonation	Greeting people; Meeting new people
Unit 2 All about me					
Getting started Talk about objects					
2A	Talk about your hometown	*be*: *it's* / *it's not*; Possessive adjectives	Common adjectives; *in* / *near*	Sound and spelling: /h/ and /w/	
2B	Talk about possessions and common objects	Plural nouns; *I have* / *you have*; *a* / *an*	Common objects 1; Numbers 1	Sound and spelling: /s/, /z/, /ɪz/; *Do you … ?*	
2C	Ask for and give personal information			Stressed parts in questions; Intonation in questions	Asking for and giving personal information
Unit 3 Food and drink					
Getting started Talk about the food in a shopping cart					
3A	Say what you eat and drink	Simple present: *I* / *you* / *we* / *they*	Food 1	Syllables and word stress; Sound and spelling: /i/, /ɪ/, and /ɑɪ/	
3B	Talk about food and meals	Adverbs of frequency	Food 2; Time; *What time* / *When … ?*	Sound and spelling: /æ/ and /ɔ/	
3C	Order and pay in a café			Syllable stress; Stressed and unstressed words	Ordering and paying in a café
Unit 4 My life and my family					
Getting started Talk about who people are and what they do					
4A	Talk about your life and ask about others'	Simple present: *Wh-* questions	Common verbs; *study*	Stressed words	
4B	Talk about your family	Simple present: *he* / *she* / *it* affirmative	Family and people; Numbers 2; *How old … ?*	Sound and spelling: /ð/	
4C	Ask and talk about photos			Sound and spelling: /ʧ/ and /ʤ/	Asking and talking about photos
Unit 5 Places					
Getting started Talk about an unusual museum					
5A	Describe a town	*there is* / *there are*: affirmative	Places in a town; *a few*, *a lot of*	*there's* / *there are*; Sound and spelling: /u/ and /ʌ/	
5B	Talk about hotels and hostels	*there is* / *there are*: negative and questions	Hotels	Sound and spelling: /ʃ/; Stressed syllables	
5C	Ask about and say where places are			Emphasizing what you say 1	Asking and saying where places are
Unit 6 Work and routines					
Getting started Talk about a job					
6A	Talk about people's jobs	Simple present: *he* / *she* / *it* negative	Jobs; *work* / *job*	Main stress in compound nouns; Sound and spelling: /ʃ/ and /ʧ/	
6B	Talk about daily routines and habits	Simple present: *he* / *she* / *it* questions	Daily routine; *for*, *from … to …* , *until*	Consonant clusters; Sentence stress	
6C	Make and accept offers			*would*; Emphasizing what you say 2	Making and accepting offers

Phonemic symbols and Irregular verbs p. 103   **Communication Plus** p. 104   **Grammar Focus** p. 116   **Vocabulary Focus** p. 136

2

Contents

Listening	Reading	Speaking	Writing
A conversation about who you are	Three conversations meeting other students	Who you are and where you're from	
A conversation about people in pictures		People in a picture	
First day at work	An online profile	Greeting and meeting new people	A personal profile; Capital letters and periods
			Unit Progress Test
Three conversations about hometowns	Three posts: *Our Homes*	Homes and hometowns	My hometown; A friend's home
A conversation at the airport		Possessions; What's in the bag?	
Finding a new apartment	A personal information form	Asking for and giving personal information	A personal information form; Spelling
			Unit Progress Test
A conversation about food likes and dislikes	Three families' weekly food: *Food for One Week*	Food likes and dislikes	
Three conversations about dinner	An article: *The Number One Breakfast in …*	Saying the time; Meal times and what you eat	
In a café	A text message	Ordering and paying in a café	A text message; Contractions
			Unit Progress Test
A conversation about work and travel to work	A blog: *Breakfast in Málaga and Lunch in London*	Work, home, and study	About you
Photos of famous people and their families	Photo captions; *An International Family*	Your family	
Talking about family photos	A photo caption	Photos	Photo captions; Word order
			Unit Progress Test
A conversation about places in a town	An article: *Very hot! Very cold!*	A street in your town	On my street
A conversation at a hostel reception	A hostel review	Hotels and hostels	Questions about a town
Looking for a café	An email	Places in a town	About your town; *and* and *but*
			Unit Progress Test
Four people talk about their jobs	A website: *Jobs International*	People's jobs	Questions about jobs
A conversation about taking photos at night	An article: *A Good Night's Sleep*	People's daily routines and habits	Questions about daily routines
A friend's birthday	An email about daily life	Offering to pay for food and drink	An email about daily life; *because* and *also*
			Unit Progress Test

Writing Plus p. 158

3

This page is intentionally left blank.

This page is intentionally left blank.

CLASSROOM LANGUAGE

Listen.

Read.

Write.

Watch.

Teacher

Look at the pictures.

Work in pairs.

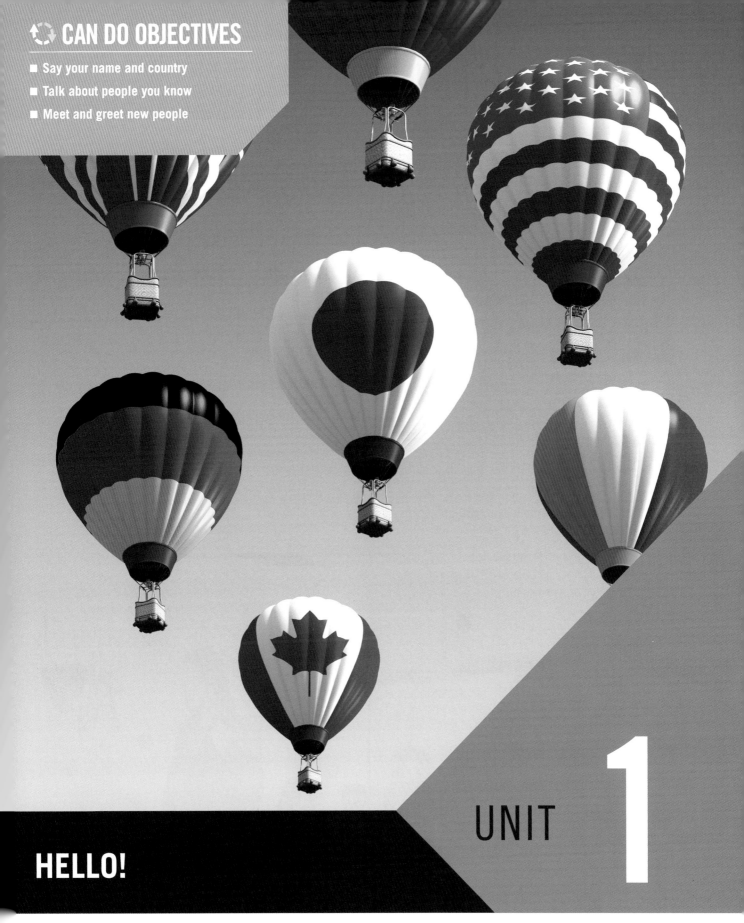

UNIT 1

HELLO!

GETTING STARTED

a 💬 Look at the picture. What country flags do you see?

b 💬 What other countries do you know in English?

1A | I'M FROM MEXICO

1 READING AND GRAMMAR

be: *I* / *you* / *we* affirmative and questions

a ▶ 01.01 Listen. Then say *Hi, I'm …* or *Hello, I'm …* and say your name.

Hi, I'm Rubén.

Hello, I'm Harumi.

b ▶ 01.02 Read and listen to conversations 1–3. Match the conversations with groups of people a–c in the picture below.

c Complete the sentences in the chart.

I/we	you
I _____ Camila. (= *I am …*) We _____ from Ecuador. (= *we are …*)	_____ you from the U.S.? How _____ you?

d ≫ Now go to Grammar Focus 1A Part 1 on p. 116.

e Sound and spelling *I'm, we're*

  1 ▶ 01.06 Listen to the sound of *I'm* and *we're*.
     a I am   b I'm   c we are   d we're
  2 💬 Practice saying *I'm* and *we're*.

f 💬 Practice the conversations in 1b.
  1 Work in pairs. Practice Conversation 1.
  2 Work in groups of three. Practice Conversation 2.
  3 Work with a new partner. Practice Conversation 3.

g 💬 Practice the conversations in 1b again. Use your own name.

1
V Hi, I'm Vilma. What's your name?
C I'm Camila.
V Hi, Camila. Nice to meet you.

2
H Hello, I'm Harumi.
K Hi. I'm Katia.
P And I'm Pablo. Hi.
H Are you from the U.S.?
P No, we're from Ecuador.

3
L Hi, Rubén. How are you?
R Hi, Li. I'm fine. How are you?
L Fine, thanks.

Kelly

Michael

2 LISTENING AND GRAMMAR *be: I / you / we* negative

a ▶ 01.07 Read and listen to the conversation. Choose the correct answers.

KELLY Are you Rubén?
RUBÉN Yes, I am.
KELLY Hi, I'm Kelly.
RUBÉN Oh, hi. Are you a student here?
KELLY No, I'm not a student. I'm your teacher!
RUBÉN Oh … sorry.

1 Rubén is:
   a a student.   **b** a teacher.
2 Kelly is:
   a a student.   **b** a teacher.

b Complete the sentences in the chart.

Affirmative (+)	Negative (–)
I'm___ a student. (= *I am*)	I'm _____ a student. (= *I am not*)
We _____ from England. (= *we are*)	We're not from England. (= *we are not*)

c ≫ Now go to Grammar Focus 1A Part 2 on p. 116.

d Read the sentences. Make them true for you.
   1 I'm a student.
   2 We're teachers.
   3 I'm from the U.S.
   4 I'm Laura.
   5 We're from Tokyo.

e 💬 Tell a partner your sentences in 2d. Are they the same?

3 VOCABULARY AND READING Countries

a ▶ 01.09 Match the countries in the box with maps 1–8. Listen and check.

the United Kingdom / the U.K.   China   the United States / the U.S.   Spain   Japan   Ecuador   Brazil   Mexico

b ▶ 01.10 Complete the sentences with the correct country. Listen and check.

OUR GROUP

Vilma 17:02
I'm Vilma. I'm from Rio de Janeiro, in ¹_____.

Pablo 17:02
Hi, I'm Pablo. I'm from ²_____. I'm from Cuenca.

Camila 17:03
Hello. I'm from Puebla, in ³_____, and my name's Camila.

Li 17:03
Hi, I'm Li. I'm from Beijing, in ⁴_____. But I'm not in Beijing now. I'm a student in Shanghai.

Harumi 17:03
My name's Harumi. I'm from Tokyo, in ⁵_____.

Michael 17:03
I'm Michael. I'm from ⁶_____. I'm a teacher in London.

Rubén 17:03
I'm from Barcelona, in ⁷_____, and my name's Rubén.

Kelly 17:03
Hello. I'm a teacher, and my name's Kelly. I'm from New York, in ⁸_____.

c ≫ Now go to Vocabulary Focus 1A on p. 136.

d Choose a city and a country in 3a. Write it on a piece of paper.

Puebla, Mexico

e 💬 Give your piece of paper to the teacher and take a new one. Try to find the student with the information on your piece of paper.

Are you from Puebla?
No, I'm not. I'm from Mexico City.

4 SPEAKING

≫ **Communication 1A**

Student A go to p. 104.
Student B go to p. 106.

1B | HE'S ECUADORIAN

Learn to talk about people you know

G be: he / she / they
V Nationalities

1 VOCABULARY Nationalities

a 💬 Do you know the people in pictures a–h?
Ask your partner.

> Do you know Serena
> and Venus Williams?

b Match the nationalities with pictures a–h.

A|mer|i|can Chi|nese Mex|i|can Ec|ua|do|ri|an
Span|ish Brit|ish Jap|a|nese Bra|zil|ian

c ▶ 01.12 Pronunciation Listen to the words in 1b.
How many syllables are in each word?
A|mer|i|can = 4 syllables

d ▶ 01.13 Listen and notice the stressed syllable.

e ▶ 01.12 Listen to the words in 1b again. Underline
the stressed syllables. Then listen and repeat.

f ≫ Now go to Vocabulary Focus 1B on p. 136.

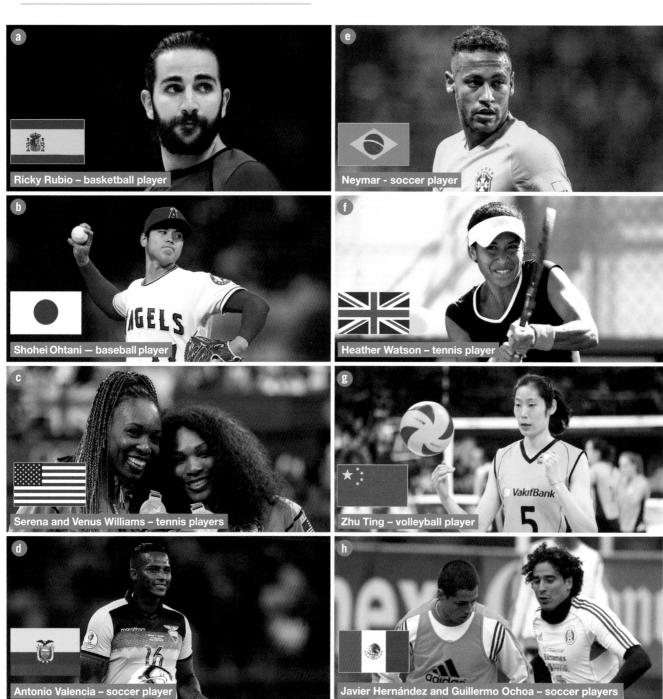

a — Ricky Rubio – basketball player
e — Neymar - soccer player
b — Shohei Ohtani — baseball player
f — Heather Watson – tennis player
c — Serena and Venus Williams – tennis players
g — Zhu Ting – volleyball player
d — Antonio Valencia – soccer player
h — Javier Hernández and Guillermo Ochoa – soccer players

2 GRAMMAR *be: he / she / they* affirmative

a ▶ 01.15 Match 1–3 with a–c. Listen and check.

1 Heather Watson is a tennis player.
2 Shohei Ohtani is a baseball player.
3 Serena and Venus Williams are tennis players.

a He's Japanese.
b They're American.
c She's British.

b Complete the chart.

+
she is … she's …
he is … ¹ _____ …
they are … ² _____ …

c ⟫ Now go to Grammar Focus 1B Part 1 on p. 116.

d Write two sentences about the people below.

1 Ricky Rubio
2 Zhu Ting
3 Javier Hernández and Guillermo Ochoa

e 💬 Tell a partner your sentences in 2d. Are they the same?

3 LISTENING

a ▶ 01.17 Look at the photo below. Read and listen to Mia talk about the people on her vacation. Complete 1–6 with the words in the box.

American	Luis	Lucía	Colombian	Mexican	Anna

MIA This is ¹ _____. She's my friend from Chicago. She's ² _____.
NOAH OK. And who's this?
MIA This is ³ _____. He's a teacher in Brazil.
NOAH Is he Brazilian?
MIA No, he's not Brazilian. He's ⁴ _____.
NOAH Oh, really.
MIA And these are my friends ⁵ _____ and Mateo. They're married.
NOAH Are they American?
MIA No, they're not American. They're ⁶ _____ – from Veracruz.

b 💬 Tell a partner about two of your friends. What nationality are they?

4 GRAMMAR

be: he / she / they negative and questions

a Complete the charts with the words in the box.

they	's not	is	are	're not	she

+	−
She's Spanish. They're Chinese.	She _____ Spanish. They _____ Chinese.

?
_____ _____ Spanish?
_____ _____ Chinese?

b ⟫ Now go to Grammar Focus 1B Part 2 on p. 116.

c ▶ 01.21 Complete the sentences. Listen and check.

1 **A** _____ he Mexican?
   B No, _____ _____.
2 **A** _____ they American?
   B Yes, _____ _____.
3 **A** _____ she Chinese?
   B No, _____ _____.
4 **A** _____ they Brazilian?
   B No, _____ _____.
5 **A** _____ he British?
   B Yes, _____ _____.

d 💬 Practice saying 1–5 in 4c with a partner.

Language Plus *this / these*

This is Anna.
this = one person

These are my friends Lucía and Mateo.
these = two or more people

5 SPEAKING

⟫ **Communication 1B** Student A go to p. 104. Student B go to p. 106.

1C EVERYDAY ENGLISH
Nice to meet you

Learn to meet and greet new people
P Intonation
W A personal profile

1 LISTENING

a 💬🔊 Look at picture a. Is she in an office?

b ▶01.22 Listen to Part 1 and check your answer in 1a.

c ▶01.22 Listen to Part 1 again. Complete the sentences with words in the box.

Hi   Good morning

RECEPTIONIST _____, welcome to Blue Web Technology.
SOPHIA _____, my name's Sophia Taylor. It's my first day.

2 USEFUL LANGUAGE Greeting people

a Complete 1–3 with the words in the box.

evening   morning   afternoon

7 a.m.–12 p.m. = ¹_____
12 p.m.–5 p.m. = ²_____
5 p.m.–10 p.m. = ³_____

b ▶01.23 **Pronunciation** Listen. How many syllables are in the words and expressions?

hi (1)   good|mor|ning   good|eve|ning
hel|lo   good|af|ter|noon

c ▶01.23 Listen to the words and expressions in 2b again. Underline the stressed syllables.

hel<u>lo</u>

d 💬🔊 Look at the times with a partner. Use the correct expression.

1 8 p.m.   3 11 a.m.   5 6 a.m.
2 3 p.m.   4 10 p.m.   6 1 p.m.

Good morning.

Good afternoon.

3 LISTENING AND USEFUL LANGUAGE
Meeting new people 1

a ▶01.24 Listen to Part 2. Sophia meets the manager of Blue Web Technology. What's his name?

☐ Daniel   ☐ Darren   ☐ David

b ▶01.25 Listen to the sentences. <u>Underline</u> the words you hear. Are both options in 1–2 possible?

1 *I'm / My name's* Sophia Taylor.
2 *I'm / My name's* David.

c ▶01.26 **Pronunciation** Listen and notice the stressed words.

A How are <u>you</u>?
B I'm <u>good</u>, thank you. And <u>you</u>?
A I'm <u>fine</u>, thanks.

d Practice the conversation in 3c with a partner.

e ▶01.27 Listen to the expressions. Complete them with the words in the box.

not bad   I'm   morning   thank you

1 **A** How are you?
  B I'm fine, ¹_____
  _____.

2 **A** Hi! How are you?
  B Oh, ²_____ _____, thanks.

3 **A** My name's Jack.
  B ³_____ Chloe.

4 **A** Good ⁴_____. How are you?
  B I'm OK, thank you.

f 💬🔊 Practice the conversations in 3e with a partner.

4 LISTENING AND USEFUL LANGUAGE Meeting new people 2

a ▶ 01.28 Listen to Part 3. Are Sophia and Isaac friends?

b ▶ 01.28 Listen to Part 3 again. Underline the correct answer.
1 **ISAAC**   Nice to *meet* / *see* you too, Sophia.
2 **DAVID**   So, this is your *home* / *office*.
3 **ISAAC**   OK. So, ... this is your *desk* / *chair*.

c ▶ 01.29 Put the conversation in the correct order. Listen and check.
☐ **ISAAC**   Nice to meet you, too, Sophia.
☐ **SOPHIA**   Nice to meet you, Isaac.
☐ **DAVID**   This is Isaac Jackson.

d Work in groups of three. Practice the conversation in 4c. Use your names.

This is Hassan.

Nice to meet you, Hassan.

5 PRONUNCIATION Intonation

a ▶ 01.30 Listen to phrases 1–5. Does the intonation change or stay the same →?
1 Hello.   3 I'm good.   5 Thank you.
2 How are you?   4 Nice to meet you.

b ▶ 01.30 Listen to the phrases in 5a again and repeat.

6 SPEAKING

a ▶ 01.31 Complete the conversation. Listen and check.

MICHELLE	Hi.
LEE	Good afternoon.
JORGE	Hello.
MICHELLE	I'm Michelle, and this [1]_____ Lee.
JORGE	Nice to meet you. I'm Jorge.
LEE	Nice to [2]_____ you, too. How are you?
JORGE	I'm good. And [3]_____ ?
LEE	I'm good.
MICHELLE	I'm [4]_____, too.

b Work in groups of three. Practice the conversation in 6a. Use your names.

7 WRITING

a Read Sophia's profile. What information about her is new?

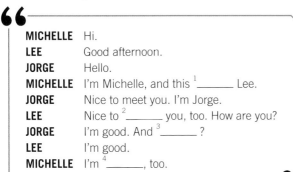

BLUE WEB TECHNOLOGY

Our people in Atlanta

Hi, my name's Sophia Taylor. I'm from Toronto in Canada. I'm in an office with Isaac Jackson.

b Now go to Writing Plus 1C on p. 158 for Capital letters and periods.

c Write a profile about you and your English class. Here are some ideas:
Hi/Hello, my ...
I'm from ... in ...
I'm in a class with ... in room ...

d Read other students' profiles. Is everyone from the same place?

◇ UNIT PROGRESS TEST

→ CHECK YOUR PROGRESS

YOU CAN NOW DO THE UNIT PROGRESS TEST.

UNIT 1
Review

1 GRAMMAR

a Underline the correct answer.

1 Hello. I *'m* / *are* Anna.
2 "Are you students?" "Yes, *we're* / *we are*."
3 You *am not* / *'re not* a teacher.
4 "*Am I* / *I am* right?" "Yes, you are."
5 Where *are you* / *you are*?
6 We *'re* / *am* at home.

b Add *is*, *'s not*, *are*, or *'re not*.

1 "Is your name Sandy?" "No, it _____."
2 "Are Javier Hernández and Guillermo Ochoa from Mexico?"
  "Yes, they _____."
3 "Is Ricky Rubio Spanish?" "Yes, he _____."
4 "_____ New York and Washington in the U.S.?"
  "Yes, they are."
5 "Are your friends soccer players?" "No, they _____."
6 "_____ your teacher English?"
  "No, she _____."

c 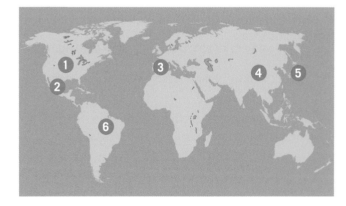 Ask and answer the questions in 1b.

d Correct the sentences.

> They's Spanish.
  They're Spanish.

1 No, he 're not from China.   4 She is Colombian?
2 You are OK?   5 I not am Brazilian.
3 Yes, I'm.   6 They are from the U.S.?

2 VOCABULARY

a Write the names of the countries.

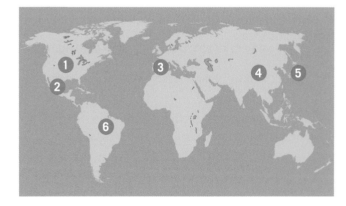

1 e n d i U t s S a t t e _____
2 e i x M c o _____
3 i p S a n _____
4 h i C a n _____
5 a n a J p _____
6 l a r B i z _____

b Complete the nationalities.

> Spa <u>nish</u> _____

1 Canad_____

4 Jap_____

2 Brazil_____

5 Brit_____

3 Amer_____

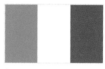
6 Ital_____

3 SOUND AND SPELLING

a Write the short forms in the chart.

Full forms	Short forms
I am	I'm
They are	They're
She is	_____
We are	_____
It is	_____
I am not	_____ not
He is not	He _____

b ▶ 01.32 Listen and practice saying the short forms.

c ▶ 01.33 Listen to these phrases. <u>Underline</u> the stressed word or syllable.

1 Good <u>morning</u>.
2 How are you?
3 They're American.
4 We're teachers.
5 Nice to meet you.

d ▶ 01.33 Listen again to check. Practice saying the sentences.

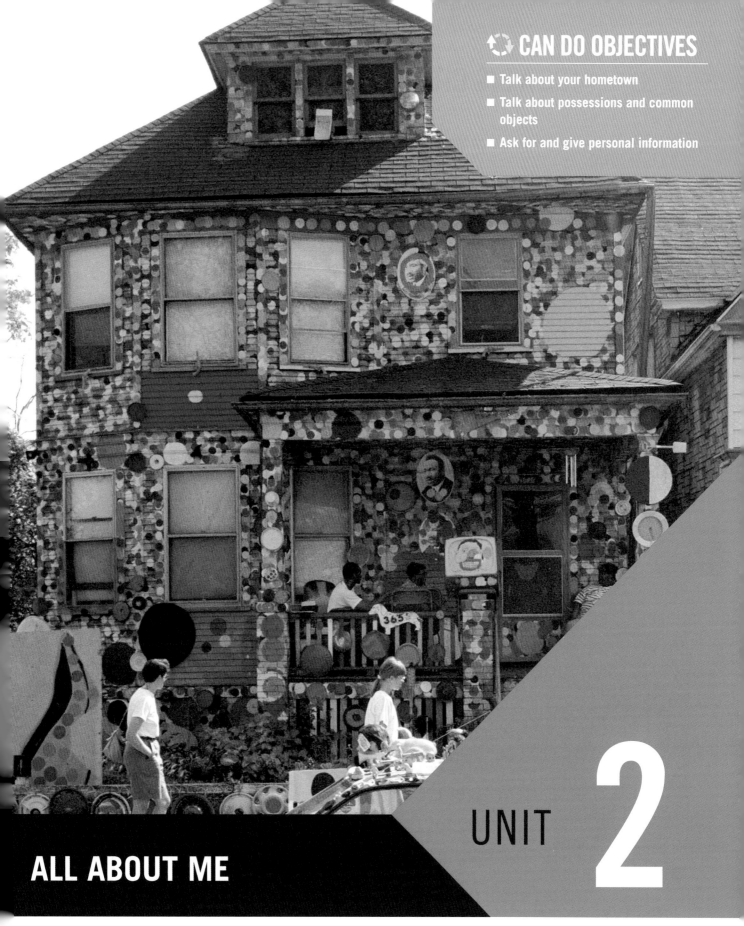

♻ CAN DO OBJECTIVES

■ Talk about your hometown
■ Talk about possessions and common objects
■ Ask for and give personal information

UNIT **2**

ALL ABOUT ME

GETTING STARTED

a 💬 Look at the picture and answer the questions.

1 Is it a … ?
  • hot country
  • big city
  • new house
2 What country do you think it is?

3 Count (1, 2, 3, …):
  • the windows on the house
  • the people in the picture

b 💬 What colors do you see on the house?

2A | IT'S A BIG CITY

Learn to talk about your hometown
- **G** *be: it's / it's not*; Possessive adjectives
- **V** Common adjectives

1 LISTENING

a ▶ 02.01 Match the words in the box with pictures a–b. Listen and check.

town   city

💬 Which are you from?

b ▶ 02.02 Listen and match pictures a–b with the names in the box.

Rocío   Carlo

c ▶ 02.02 Listen again. Complete the sentences with the words in the box.

is   it   it's   it's not

Conversation 1
A Is ¹_____ a big city?
B No, no. ²_____ a city.
Conversation 2
A ³_____ it a city?
B Yes, it is. _____⁴ a big city.

2 GRAMMAR *be: it's / it's not*

a Complete the chart with *it* or *it's*.

+	Ravello is in Italy.	_____ in Italy.
–	Ravello's not in Mexico.	_____ not in Mexico.
?	Is Ravello in Italy?	Is _____ in Italy?

b Complete the sentences with *he's*, *she's*, or *it's*.
1 Giovanna's from Ravello in Italy. _____ a town near Naples.
2 Aaron's from Blue Bell, Pennsylvania. _____ American.
3 Ricardo's Spanish. _____ from Madrid.
4 Akira's from Sōka in Japan. _____ a city near Tokyo.
5 Vanessa's from Zapopan in Mexico. _____ a big city near Guadalajara.

c ▶ 02.03 Listen and check.

d ≫ Now go to Grammar Focus 2A Part 1 on p. 118.

Language Plus *in / near*

*Naples is **in** Italy.*   *Ravello is **near** Naples.*

Naples

Naples
Ravello

e Write sentences about you.
I'm from …   It's a (town / city) (in / near) …

f 💬 Tell a partner your sentences.

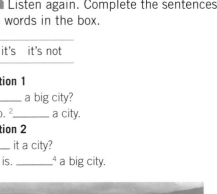

a

b

3 READING AND VOCABULARY
Common adjectives

a ▶ 02.06 Read and listen to *Our Homes*. Complete the chart.

	home		home
Rocío	*big apartment*	Miguel	
Carlo		Pietro and Susanna	
Aaron		Sophia	

b Sound and spelling /h/ and /w/

1 ▶ 02.07 Listen to the words. Which words have a /h/ sound? Which words have a /w/ sound?

home	hi	who	what	how	hotel	where

2 💬🗩 Practice saying the words.

c ▶ 02.08 Complete the sentences with the words in the box. Listen and check.

big	small	old	new

1 It's a _____ house. 2 It's a _____ apartment.

3 It's a _____ city. 4 It's an _____ house.

d ≫ Now go to Vocabulary Focus 2A on p. 137.

4 GRAMMAR
Possessive adjectives

a Read *Our Homes* again. Complete the chart.

Pronoun	Possessive adjective
I	_____
you	*your*
he	_____
she	*her*
we	*our*
they	_____

Our ⌂⌂⌂
Homes
||||||||||||||||||||||||||||||||

My apartment is in a new part of Quito. It's very big. My friend Miguel is from Otavalo. It's a beautiful town near Quito. This is his home – it's a small house. **Rocío**

My apartment in Ravello is big, old, and beautiful. My friends Pietro and Susanna are from Naples. This is their home. It's a big apartment in a nice part of town. **Carlo**

My home is a small house in Blue Bell. It's an old town. My friend Sophia is from Philadelphia. This is her home. It's a small apartment, and it's new and beautiful. **Aaron**

b Complete the sentences.

1 Javier is from Barcelona. _____ home is in a nice part of the city.
2 Are you from Berlin? Where's _____ apartment?
3 We're from Bogotá. _____ home is near a big hotel.
4 Sarah is from England. _____ town is near Hastings.
5 Pedro and Eva are from Mexico City. _____ apartment is very big.

c ≫ Now go to Grammar Focus 2A Part 2 on p. 118.

d Complete the sentences about a friend.

My friend _____ is from _____. His / Her home is _____.

e 💬🗩 Tell a partner about your friend's home.

5 SPEAKING

≫ Communication 2A

Student A go to p. 104.
Student B go to p. 106.
Student C go to p. 108.

2B | DO YOU HAVE A PHONE?

Learn to talk about possessions and common objects

G Plural nouns; *have*

V Common objects 1; Numbers 1

1 VOCABULARY Common objects 1

a ▶ 02.11 Match 1–10 in picture a with the words in the box. Listen and check.

> a computer   a newspaper   a knife   a phone   a key
> a watch   an umbrella   a ticket   a book   a bottle of water

b 💬 Two objects in 1a are not OK at an airport. What are they?

Language Plus *a / an*

We use *a* before most nouns.   • *a key*   • *a book*
We use *an* before *a, e, i, o, u.*   • *an apple*   • *an umbrella*

c 💬 Cover the words in the box in 1a. Ask a partner questions about the objects in the picture.

What's this?

It's a watch.

d ≫ Now go to Vocabulary Focus 2B Common objects 1 on p. 138.

2 LISTENING AND GRAMMAR Plural nouns

a ▶ 02.13 Listen to the conversation with an airport customs official. Check (✓) the words you hear.

- ☐ books
- ☐ computers
- ☐ phones
- ☐ watches
- ☐ umbrellas
- ☐ bottles
- ☐ newspapers
- ☐ knives

b Complete the chart.

Singular (= 1)	Plural (= 2+)
a key	keys
a newspaper	＿＿＿
a watch	＿＿＿
a knife	＿＿＿

c Most nouns add *-s* in the plural. How are the plurals of *watch* and *knife* different?

18

d 💬🔊 **Sound and spelling** /s/, /z/, and /ɪz/

> 1 ▶️ **02.14** Listen and practice these sounds. Which word has an extra syllable in the plural?
> 1 /s/ book**s**   2 /z/ key**s**   3 /ɪz/ watch**es**
>
> 2 ▶️ **02.15** Listen to these words. Which word has an extra syllable in the plural? Listen again and repeat.
>
> knives   bottles   tickets   apples   houses   phones

e 💬🔊 Work in pairs.

Student A: Say a singular word.
Student B: Say the plural.

Then switch roles.

f ≫ Now go to Grammar Focus 2B on p. 118.

3 GRAMMAR *I have / you have*

a ▶️ **02.16** Look at the X-ray picture and complete the conversation. Listen and check.

A What's in your bag?
B Mm, I have a ¹b_____, and my ²k_____s, and an ³u_____.
A Do you have a ⁴p_____?
B Yes. Oh, and a ⁵b_____of w_____. Sorry!

b ▶️ **02.17** Listen to the forms of *have*.

+	?
I **have** a book.	**Do** you **have** a book?

c ▶️ **02.17** **Pronunciation** Listen again. Practice saying the sentences.

d 💬🔊 Ask a partner about objects 1–5 in 3a. Ask about:

1 here (in class)
2 at home

> Do you have an umbrella here?
> No.
> Do you have an umbrella at home?
> Yes.

4 VOCABULARY Numbers 1

a ▶️ **02.18** Listen and repeat the numbers.

b Match the words in the box with numbers 1–12 in 4a.

> seven   two   nine   four   eight   eleven
> three   six   one   ten   twelve   five

c 💬🔊 Work in pairs.

Student A: Say a number.
Student B: Say the next number.

Then switch roles.

d ≫ **Communication 2B** Student A go to p. 104. Student B go to p. 106.

e ≫ Now go to Vocabulary Focus 2B Numbers 1 on p. 141.

5 SPEAKING

a Write three things you have in your bag.

a bottle of water

an apple   *a computer*

b 💬🔊 Guess what is in your partner's bag.

> Do you have a phone?
> Yes.
> Do you have a knife?
> No!

2C EVERYDAY ENGLISH
What's your address?

Learn to ask for and give personal information
- **p** Intonation in questions
- **w** A form

1 LISTENING

a Think about a good home for you. Check (✓) <u>four</u> boxes.

1. ☐ a house
   ☐ an apartment
2. ☐ in a small town
   ☐ in a city
3. ☐ big
   ☐ small
4. ☐ near a park
   ☐ near stores

b 💬 Tell a partner about your home in 1a.

> A good home for me is …

c ▶️02.21 Listen to Part 1. Answer the questions.

1. Who asks questions, Juan or the woman?
2. What kind of home does Juan need, an apartment or a house?

d ▶️02.21 Listen to Part 1 again. Check (✓) the correct answer.

1. Juan's last name:
   a ☐ Hays   b ☐ Hayes
2. His address in Seattle:
   a ☐ 55 Park Street   b ☐ 5 Park Street
3. His phone number:
   a ☐ 760 264 7893   b ☐ 760 264 7389

2 USEFUL LANGUAGE Asking for and giving personal information

a ▶️02.22 <u>Underline</u> the correct answer. Listen and check.

1. **A** What's your last name?
   B *It's / I'm* Robinson.
2. **A** What's your address?
   B *It's / It's on* 7 King Street.
3. **A** What's your phone number?
   B *They're / It's* 421 505 2738.
4. **A** What's your email address?
   B *He's / It's* chrisrobinson@travelmail.com.

b ▶️02.23 Listen to the answers to questions 3 and 4 in 2a again. Check (✓) the correct answer.

1. a ☐ four-two-one-five-oh-five-two-seven-three-eight
   b ☐ four-two-fifteen-oh-five-two-seven-three-eight

2. a ☐ chris-robinson-from-travelmail-point-com
   b ☐ chris-robinson-at-travelmail-dot-com

c ▶️02.24 <u>Underline</u> the correct word. Listen and check your answer.

AGENT Juan Hayes. *What / How* do you spell that?
JUAN J-U-A-N.

d ▶️02.25 **Pronunciation** Listen to the questions. Notice the stressed part in each question.

1. How do you <u>spell</u> that?
2. Can you <u>spell</u> that?
3. Sorry, what's the <u>spelling</u>?

▶️02.25 Listen again and repeat.

e ≫ Now go to Writing Plus 2C Part 1 on p. 158 for The alphabet.

f 💬 Ask a partner his/her last name. Then ask how to spell it.

g ≫ **Communication 2C** Student A go to p. 105. Student B go to p. 108.

3 LISTENING

a ▶ 02.27 Listen to Part 2. What does Juan think? Check (✓) the correct sentence.

1 ☐ The apartment's really nice.
2 ☐ The apartment's not very nice.

b ▶ 02.27 Listen to Part 2 again. Check (✓) the correct information about the apartment.

1 ☐ small   ☐ big
2 ☐ good for one person   ☐ good for two people
3 ☐ near a supermarket   ☐ near a park

4 PRONUNCIATION Intonation in questions

a ▶ 02.28 Listen to the questions. Does the intonation go up ↗ or down ↘ at the end?

1 What's your last name?
2 What's your phone number?

b ▶ 02.28 Listen again and repeat the questions.

c 💬 ▶ 02.29 Practice asking the questions with a partner. Then listen and check the intonation.

1 What's your address?   3 What's the spelling?
2 Where are you from?

5 SPEAKING

a 💬 Talk to different students. Ask about:

• names (first name and last name)   • address
• phone number   • email address

Write down the information. Ask about the spelling.

What's your last name?

It's Mishkin.

Can you spell that, please?

M-I-S-H-K-I-N.

6 WRITING

a Read about Juan. What's the new information?

Local Rentals: Customer Information

First name:	Juan
Last name:	Hayes
Address:	55 Park Street
Phone number:	760 264 7893
Email:	juanh@travelmail.com

b ≫ Now go to Writing Plus 2C Part 2 on p. 158 for Spelling.

c Complete the form with your information.

Local Rentals: Customer Information

First name:	
Last name:	
Address:	
Phone number:	
Email:	

☑ UNIT PROGRESS TEST

→ CHECK YOUR PROGRESS

YOU CAN NOW DO THE UNIT PROGRESS TEST.

UNIT 2
Review

1 GRAMMAR

a Correct the <u>underlined</u> word.

> <u>It's</u> big houses. *They're*
1 This is Katia, and this is <u>she</u> house.
2 "Excuse me! Is this <u>you</u> bag?" "Yes, it is! Thank you."
3 Hiro's from Sōka. <u>She's</u> a city in Japan.
4 <u>It</u> not a big apartment.
5 They live in Madrid. This is <u>they</u> home.
6 "Hi, we're from New York. <u>We</u> city is big!"

b Complete the sentences with the plural form of the nouns in parentheses.

1 They're my _____. (key)
2 Are they your _____? (knife)
3 I have two _____. (watch)
4 Are they your _____? (bottle of water)
5 San Francisco and Seattle are _____ in the U.S. (city)
6 Where are the _____? (book)

c Complete the sentences with the words in the box.

---
are   his   is   they
they're   it's   it's not
---

1 I'm from Ravello. _____ a town in Italy.
2 The men _____ at home.
3 "Are they big houses?" "Yes, _____ are."
4 _____ my books.
5 _____ it a city?
6 This is John and this is _____ apartment.
7 "Is Madrid in Italy?" "No, _____."

2 VOCABULARY

a Match 1–6 with the opposite adjectives in the box.

---
boring   difficult   good
happy   old   ~~small~~   wrong

> big   small
1 easy   _____
2 bad   _____
3 right   _____
4 sad   _____
5 interesting _____
6 new   _____

b Complete the crossword with the objects in pictures 1–8.

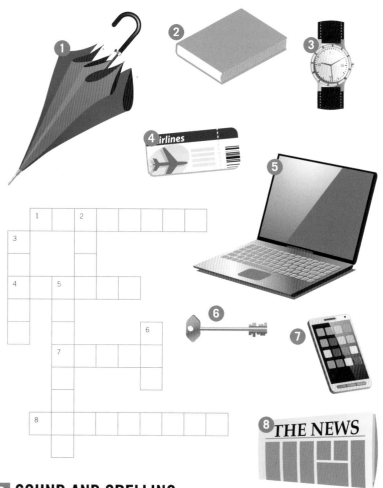

3 SOUND AND SPELLING

a ▶02.31 Look at the words in the box. Is the final sound /s/, /z/, or /ɪz/? Complete the chart. Practice saying the words.

~~phones~~   watches   keys   addresses   houses
apartments   umbrellas   tickets   books   computers

/s/	/z/	/ɪz/
	phones	

b ▶02.32 Check (✓) the words with a /h/ sound. Practice saying the words.

- [ ] hello
- [ ] her
- [ ] our
- [ ] his
- [ ] is
- [ ] home
- [ ] house
- [ ] where
- [ ] how
- [ ] who
- [ ] she
- [ ] phone
- [ ] watch
- [ ] happy
- [ ] right

⟳ REVIEW YOUR PROGRESS

How well did you do in this unit? Write 3, 2, or 1 for each objective.
3 = very well   2 = well   1 = not so well

I CAN ...	
talk about my hometown	☐
talk about possessions and common objects	☐
ask for and give personal information	☐

CAN DO OBJECTIVES

- Say what you eat and drink
- Talk about food and meals
- Order and pay in a café

UNIT 3

FOOD AND DRINK

GETTING STARTED

a 💬 Look at the picture and answer the questions.

   1 What food can you see in the shopping cart?
   2 Which food in the shopping cart do you like?

3 Which food in the shopping cart don't you like?
4 What food do you buy?

b 💬 What other food do you know in English?

23

3A DO YOU LIKE FISH?

1 VOCABULARY Food 1

a ▶03.01 Match pictures 1–7 with the words in the box. Then listen and check.

fruit   rice   meat   bread   vegetables   eggs   fish

b ▶03.01 **Pronunciation** Listen to the words in 1a again. Which word has more than one syllable? Underline the stressed syllable.

c 💬 Say two things you like ☺.

I like fruit, and I like fish.

d **Sound and spelling** /i/, /ɪ/, and /aɪ/

1 ▶03.02 Listen and practice these sounds.
1 /i/ m**ea**t   2 /ɪ/ f**i**sh   3 /aɪ/ **I**'m

2 ▶03.03 Look at the words in the box. What sounds do the letters in **bold** have? Listen and add the words to the sound groups below.

big   **ea**t   nine   sister   **i**t's   m**e**   m**i**lk
China   five   h**i**s   t**ea**cher   h**i**   ch**ee**se

Sound 1 /i/	Sound 2 /ɪ/	Sound 3 /aɪ/
meat	fish	I'm

3 💬 Practice saying the words.

e Now go to Vocabulary Focus 3A on p. 139.

2 READING AND GRAMMAR

Simple present: *I / you / we / they* affirmative and negative

a Which words in 1a can you see in pictures 1–3? Which word <u>isn't</u> in the pictures?

b ▶03.06 Read and listen to texts a–c. Match them with the families in pictures 1–3.

FOOD
FOR ONE WEEK

a They eat a lot of fruit and vegetables every day. And they eat meat with rice. They like eggs, but they don't eat bread or fish. They don't like fish. They drink a lot of water.

b They eat meat and eggs every day, but they don't eat fish. And they don't eat vegetables, but they eat fruit. They really like bread.

c They eat a lot of rice and vegetables. They like fruit, and they eat bread. They don't eat fish or meat. They are vegetarians.

Tang family, China

c Complete the chart.

+			–		
I We They	eat like	meat. fish.	I We They	_____ eat _____ like	meat. fish.

d <u>Underline</u> the correct words.

1 The Tangs *eat / don't eat* fish.
2 The Delgados *eat / don't eat* bread.
3 The Donatis *like / don't like* meat.
4 The Tangs *eat / don't eat* a lot of eggs.
5 The Donatis *like / don't like* vegetables.

e 💬 Which family's food would you like to have for a week? Why?

Donati family, Italy

Delgado family, Guatemala

3 LISTENING AND GRAMMAR **Simple present:** *I / you / we / they* **questions**

a ▶ 03.07 Listen to a conversation with Rajit. Check (✓) the different food he eats.

✓	bread	☐	vegetables	☐	meat
☐	fish	☐	rice	☐	fruit

Rajit

b ▶ 03.07 Listen again. Complete the conversation.

A Rajit, what do you eat in a week?
B Oh, a lot of things. I eat rice every day, and bread. I eat a lot of fruit. I eat fish …
A ¹_____ you eat meat?
B No, I don't like meat.
A Do you ²_____ vegetables?
B Oh yes, I like vegetables. I eat a lot of vegetables.
A Do you ³_____ them every day?
B Yes. They're very good for me.

c ▶ 03.08 Complete the questions in the chart. Then listen and check.

+	–	?
I eat fish. We like fruit.	I don't eat fish. We don't like fruit.	_____ you _____ fish? _____ you _____ fruit?

d 💬 Now go to Grammar Focus 3A on p. 118.

e 💬 Practice the conversation in 3b with a partner.

4 SPEAKING

a 💬 Ask and answer questions with a partner. Complete the chart with their answers.

Do you eat meat?

Yes, (I do).

Do you eat bread every day?

No, not every day.

Do you like fish?

No, I don't like fish.

	yes / no?	every day?	like?
meat			
fish			
rice			
bread			
vegetables			
fruit			
eggs			

b 💬 Write three words for drinks. Then ask your partner questions.

Do you drink soda?

Do you like milk?

3B | I USUALLY HAVE DINNER EARLY

1 READING

a Check (✓) the boxes about your breakfast.

b 💬 Talk about your answers in 1a with a partner.

> I have coffee – I don't have ice cream.

c 💬 Look at the pictures. What's the number one breakfast in the U.S.? Make a guess below.

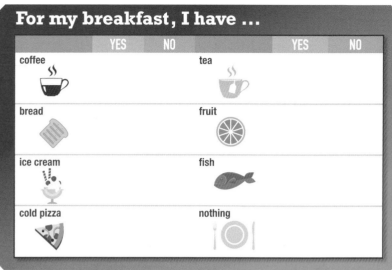

For my breakfast, I have …

	YES	NO		YES	NO
coffee			tea		
bread			fruit		
ice cream			fish		
cold pizza			nothing		

☐ fruit ☐ cereal

☐ toast ☐ eggs

d Read the text and find the answer to 1c.

THE NUMBER ONE BREAKFAST

In the U.S., people like different food for breakfast. They sometimes eat cereal with cold milk, but eggs are the number one breakfast food. They also like fruit with toast and bacon or sausage.

e 💬 What's the number one breakfast food in your country? What's the number one drink?

> I think _____ is the number one breakfast food in my country.

2 VOCABULARY Food 2; Time

a Match sentences 1–3 with pictures a–c.

1 I have lunch at *twelve* / *one* o'clock.
2 They have dinner at *six* / *seven* o'clock.
3 In my family, we have breakfast at *seven* / *eight* o'clock.

a in the morning

b in the afternoon

c in the evening

b ⟫ Now go to Vocabulary Focus 3B Food 2 on p. 140.

c ▶ 03.13 Listen to sentences 1–3 in 2a. Underline the correct words.

d ▶ 03.14 Match the clocks with the times. Listen and check.

- ☐ (a) quarter after four
- ☐ four o'clock
- ☐ (a) quarter to five
- ☐ four thirty

e 💬 Point to a clock in 2d for a partner to say the time.

f ⟫ Now go to Vocabulary Focus 3B Time on p. 141.

g **Sound and spelling** /æ/ and /ɔ/

   1 ▶ 03.16 Listen and practice these sounds.
     1 /æ/ **a**fter f**a**mily   2 /ɔ/ f**ou**r   qu**ar**ter

   2 ▶ 03.17 Look at the words in the box. What sounds do the letters in **bold** have? Listen and add the words to the sound groups below.

     cl**a**ss **a**ll **a**pple **a**fternoon w**a**ter **o**range

Sound 1 /æ/	Sound 2 /ɔ/
after	four

   3 💬 Practice saying the words.

h ⟫ **Communication 3B** Student A go to p. 105. Student B go to p. 107.

3 LISTENING

a ▶ 03.18 Listen to three people talk about dinner. Match 1–3 with a country in the box.

Ecuador Spain the U.S. Brazil Mexico China

b ▶ 03.18 Listen again. Complete the chart.

Name	Dinner time	Food
Julie		
Lucas		
Monica		

c 💬 Do you like the same food as Julie, Lucas, and Monica?

4 GRAMMAR Adverbs of frequency

a ▶ 03.19 Listen and complete the sentences with the words in the box.

always usually sometimes never

1 **JULIE**   We _____ have dinner early.
2 **LUCAS**   I _____ have fish for dinner.
3 **MONICA** People _____ have dinner early in Spain.
4 **MONICA** I _____ have bread and cheese.

b Complete 2 and 4 with words in the box in 4a.
1 always (100%)   3 sometimes (50%)
2 _____ (80%)   4 _____ (0%)

c ⟫ Now go to Grammar Focus 3B on p. 120.

d Put the words in parentheses in the correct place in the sentences.
1 I have breakfast at 9:00 on the weekends. (sometimes)
2 I have a sandwich for lunch. (usually)
3 I have breakfast. (never)
4 In the evening, I have dinner at about 7:00. (always)

e 💬 Which sentences in 4d are true for you?

Language Plus *What time ... ? / When ... ?*

What time *do you have dinner?* = **When** *do you have dinner?*

5 SPEAKING

a Answer questions 1–4. Write another question with your own idea.
1 In the morning, do you eat breakfast?
2 In the evening, do you eat a big dinner?
3 What time do you have lunch?
4 What do you eat for lunch?

b 💬 Ask and answer the questions in 5a with other students. Who has the same answers as you?

> Jaime and I never
> eat breakfast.

3C EVERYDAY ENGLISH
I'd like a large coffee, please

Learn to order and pay in a café
- **P** Stressed and unstressed words
- **W** A text message

1 LISTENING

a 💬 What food and drinks on the menu do you like? Tell a partner.

MENU

SANDWICHES
cheese, vegetable 3.00

SLICES OF PIZZA
cheese 2.50

CAKE
banana, chocolate 3.00

DRINKS
small tea, small coffee,
small orange juice 2.50
large tea, large coffee,
large bottle of water 4.00

b ▶ 03.21 **Pronunciation** Listen. This word has two syllables:

cof|fee

▶ 03.22 Which words have two syllables? Listen and check.

sandwich   banana   orange   vegetable

c ▶ 03.22 Listen to the words in 1b again. Underline the stressed syllable.

coffee

d 💬 Practice saying the words in 1b with a partner.

e Find 1–3 in pictures a–c.

1 a piece of chocolate cake   2 a watch   3 money

f ▶ 03.23 Listen. Put pictures a–c in the correct order.

g ▶ 03.23 Listen again. Are the sentences true or false?

1 Tracy has a new watch.
2 They order two large coffees.
3 Tracy likes her watch.
4 Hannah never has coffee at lunch.

2 PRONUNCIATION Stressed and unstressed words

a ▶ 03.24 Listen to 1–4. Is the pronunciation of *of* the same?

1 of   2 a piece of cake
3 a bottle of water   4 a slice of pizza

b ▶ 03.25 Listen to these phrases. Which word isn't stressed?

a large coffee   a large tea   a small orange juice

c 💬 Practice saying the phrases in 2b.

d 💬 Work in pairs. Practice more phrases with *a large / a small / a piece of* … . Use the menu in 1a or your own ideas.

3 USEFUL LANGUAGE Ordering and paying in a café

a ▶ 03.26 Listen and complete the sentences.

1 **HANNAH** I'd _____ a large coffee, please.
2 **TRACY** Can we _____ two pieces of chocolate cake, please?

▶ 03.26 Listen again and repeat.

b ▶ 03.27 Put the words in the correct order. Listen and check.

1 have / I / a small / can / coffee, / please ?
2 please / a vegetable sandwich, / I'd like .
3 two / can / have / we / banana cake / pieces of ?

c 💬 Practice saying the sentences in 3b with a partner.

d ▶ 03.28 Put the conversation in the correct order. Listen and check.

- [ ] A slice of cheese pizza, please.
- [ ] Of course. That's five dollars, please.
- [ ] Sure. And to eat?
- [ ] Here you go.
- [ ] Can I have a bottle of water, please?
- [ ] Thank you.

e 💬 Practice the conversation in 3d with a partner. Change the drink, food, and price.

> Can I have a small
> orange juice, please?

4 SPEAKING

a 💬 Work with a partner. Student A: You work in a café. Student B: You're a customer. Use the menu on p. 28 and the conversation map below.

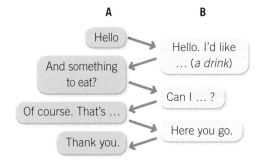

A | B
Hello → Hello. I'd like ... (a drink)
And something to eat? ← Can I ... ?
Of course. That's ... ← Here you go.
Thank you. ←

b 💬 Switch roles and repeat the conversation.

5 WRITING

a Read the text message Tracy sends from her new smartwatch. Who is it for?

> Hi, Brian. I'm at a café with Hannah. She's my friend from work. This message is from my new smartwatch. I love it! Talk to you later!
>
> Delivered

b ≫ Now go to Writing Plus 3C on p. 159 for Contractions.

c Write a text message to a friend. Here are some ideas:

Hi, ...
I'm ... (at school / at work / at a café / at a restaurant) with ...
He's / She's ... (Spanish / a student / very nice)
Talk (to you) / See you soon / later.

d Read a partner's text message. Who does he/she write about?

✓ UNIT PROGRESS TEST

→ **CHECK YOUR PROGRESS**

YOU CAN NOW DO THE UNIT PROGRESS TEST.

1 GRAMMAR

a Write simple present sentences and questions with the words and phrases.

> (–) I / have / lunch at home.
> *I don't have lunch at home.*

1 (?) you / like / eggs
2 (+) we / eat / bread every day.
3 (–) I / drink / juice.
4 (–) we / eat / meat.
5 (+) you / like / fruit.
6 (?) they / eat / fish

b Underline the correct answer.

1 *Always I* / *I always* have a sandwich for lunch.
2 I *drink sometimes* / *sometimes drink* soda.
3 I *eat usually* / *usually eat* lunch at home.
4 I *never* / *never don't* drink milk.
5 *Never I have* / *I never have* dinner at 9:00.
6 I *don't sometimes* / *sometimes don't* have breakfast.

c 💬 Are the sentences in 1b true or false for you? Tell a partner.

d Correct the sentences.

> I not like rice.
> *I don't like rice.*

1 No, we not do.
2 Always I have breakfast.
3 We not eat fish.
4 I drink usually water.
5 You like tea?
6 Yes, do I.

2 VOCABULARY

a Complete the groups with words in the box.

coffee   dinner   fish   cakes   juice   banana

1 water, milk, _____
2 tea, _____
3 orange, apple, _____
4 breakfast, lunch, _____
5 meat, eggs, _____
6 ice cream, cookies, _____

b Which is your favorite group in 2a?

c Look at 1–6 in the picture and complete the food words.

1 b_____   4 a_____s
2 r_____   5 o_____s
3 m_____   6 e_____s

3 SOUND AND SPELLING

a ▶ 03.29 Listen to the sentences. Check (✓) the sentence with the same vowel sounds in **bold**.

> T**ea**, pl**ea**se.
> a ☐ I like rice.
> b ✓ He **ea**ts m**ea**t.

1 It's a fish sandwich.
   a ☐ His big sister is six.
   b ☐ I'd like ice cream.

2 Sh**e** **ea**ts ch**ee**se.
   a ☐ Hi from China!
   b ☐ H**e** t**ea**ches m**e**.

3 Rice is nice.
   a ☐ His big sister is six.
   b ☐ I'd like ice cream.

4 Hi from China!
   a ☐ From nine to five.
   b ☐ It's a fish sandwich.

b ▶ 03.30 Listen to the words. Check (✓) the words with the /ɔ/ sound. Practice saying the words.

1 ☐ water   5 ☐ apple
2 ☐ after   6 ☐ orange
3 ☐ glass   7 ☐ quarter
4 ☐ morning   8 ☐ all

🔁 REVIEW YOUR PROGRESS

How well did you do in this unit? Write 3, 2, or 1 for each objective.
3 = very well   2 = well   1 = not so well

I CAN ...

say what I eat and drink	☐
talk about food and meals	☐
order and pay in a café	☐

UNIT 4

MY LIFE AND MY FAMILY

GETTING STARTED

a 💬 Look at the picture and answer the questions.

   1 Look at person a. Can you see … ?
   - her mother
   - her father
   - her grandparents

   2 Do you think this family all lives together in one house?

3 Who in the picture … ?
   - works
   - studies

4 What do you think the people in the picture do next?

b 💬 Who lives in your home?

Learn to ask and talk about your life
- G Simple present: *Wh-* questions
- V Common verbs

1 VOCABULARY Common verbs

a ▶ 04.01 Match sentences 1–5 with pictures a–e. Listen and check.

1 I **study** in college.
2 I **work** in an office.
3 I **speak** Japanese.
4 We **live** in Los Angeles.
5 We **go** to the gym every day.

b 💬 Which sentences in 1a are true for you?

c ≫ Now go to Vocabulary Focus 4A on p. 142.

2 READING

a Read Matt's blog. Which sentence is true?

1 "I live and I work in London."
2 "I live in Málaga, and I work in London."
3 "I speak Spanish very well."

b Read Matt's blog again. What does he say about these things?

1 apartments in London
2 beaches in Málaga
3 number of days at work (in London)
4 number of days at work (in Málaga)
5 Spanish classes
6 Málaga

c 💬 What do you think of Matt's life?

> **Language Plus** *study*
>
> ... in college
> ... at school / at an English language school
> *study* ... English / Spanish / Arabic
> ... a subject (*art, math*)

d Write sentences about you.

I live ...   I work / study ...   I study English ...

e 💬 Tell a partner your sentences in 2d.

Breakfast in MÁLAGA and Lunch in LONDON

JUST A NORMAL DAY!

I work in London.

Apartments are very expensive there. In Málaga, Spain, apartments aren't very expensive, and the beaches are beautiful. So I work in London, but I live in Málaga! I fly from Málaga to London on Monday. I work there for three days, and I stay with my sister. Then I fly to Málaga again, and I work from home two days a week. I don't speak Spanish very well, so I study Spanish at a language school and I go to classes on Saturdays. I love Málaga – it's a beautiful city, and it's great to live here!

3 LISTENING

a ▶ **04.03** Listen to Justin and Fernanda. Who lives in Ottawa, but works in Québec City?

b ▶ **04.03** Listen again. <u>Underline</u> the correct answers.

1 Fernanda is *Brazilian* / *Canadian*.
2 Her home's in *Brazil* / *Canada*.
3 Her job *is* / *isn't* near her home.
4 She *is* / *isn't* married.
5 Fernanda and Bernardo speak *English* / *Portuguese* together.

4 GRAMMAR
Simple present: *Wh-* questions

a ▶ **04.04** Complete the questions in the chart. Listen and check.

Yes/No questions	
_____ you work from home?	Yes, I work two days from home. No, I work in an office.

Wh- questions	
Where _____ you live? When _____ you have dinner? What _____ you study in college?	I live in Ottawa. I have dinner at 8:00. I study Italian.

b ≫ Now go to Grammar Focus 4A on p. 120.

c ▶ **04.07** Put the words in the correct order to make questions. Listen and check.

1 you work / do / in an office ?
2 do / where / you work ?
3 where / you live / do ?
4 college / study in / do you / what ?
5 do / speak Spanish / you ?

d ▶ **04.07** **Pronunciation** Listen to the questions in 4c again. Notice the stressed words and syllables.

1 *Do you <u>work</u> in an <u>off</u>ice?*

e ▶ **04.07** Check (✓) the words we stress. Then listen to the questions in 4c again and repeat.

1 ☐ question word (e.g., *where*)   3 ☐ main verb (e.g., *work*)
2 ☐ *do*   4 ☐ preposition (e.g., *in*)

f 💬 Ask and answer the questions in 4c with a partner.

5 SPEAKING

≫ **Communication 4A**

Student A go to p. 105.
Student B go to p. 108.

UNIT 4

4B | SHE HAS A SISTER AND A BROTHER

Learn to talk about your family

G Simple present: *he / she / it* affirmative
V Family and people; Numbers 2

1 READING AND LISTENING

a Match 1–6 with pictures a–f.

1 Soccer player Lionel Messi with his children.
2 Pop star Beyoncé with her husband, Jay-Z, and her sister Solange.
3 Movie star Kate Hudson with her parents.
4 Movie director Alejandro González Iñárritu with his wife, his son, and his daughter.
5 Actor Colin Hanks and his father, Tom Hanks.
6 Singer Camila Cabello with her mother.

b ▶ 04.08 Listen and check.

c 💬 What other things do you know about the people in the pictures?

2 VOCABULARY Family and people

a Complete the chart. Use words from 1a.

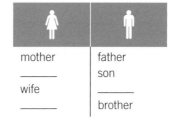

👩	👨
mother	father
————	son
wife	————
————	brother

b Which word in the sentences in 1a means … ?

1 mother and father   2 boys and girls

c Look at the family tree. Which people … ?

1 are married   3 have a sister
2 have a brother   4 have a child / children

d 💬 Work in pairs.

Student A: Choose a person from the family tree.
Student B: Ask questions to guess who Student A is.

Then switch roles.

Are you married?
    Yes.

Do you have children?
    Yes.

e ≫ Now go to Vocabulary Focus 4B Family and people on p. 143.

f **Sound and spelling** /ð/

1 ▶ 04.11 Listen and practice this sound.
/ð/ mother

2 ▶ 04.12 /ð/ is usually spelled *th*. Listen to the words and repeat.

this   that   father   they   brother   then

3 💬 Practice saying the words.

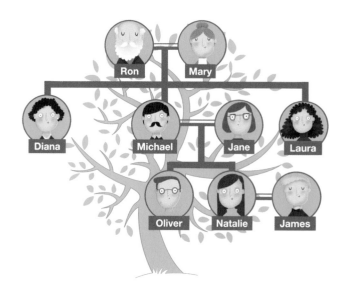

b Where do they live? Write the names of the countries.

1 Daniela   4 María
2 Carlos   5 Mehmet
3 Alex

c Daniela is forty-six. How old is … ? (Write the numbers in words.)

1 Carlos   2 Alex   3 María

Language Plus *How old … ?*

How old is *she?*
She's *25.*

How old are *her children?*
They're *three and five.*

Note: We use *be*, not *have*, to talk about age.

d ≫ Now go to Vocabulary Focus 4B Numbers 2 on p. 141.

e 💬🔊 Write the names of three famous people. How old are they? If you don't know, guess! Read out the names. What do other students think?

Lady Gaga

I think she's 38.

3 READING AND VOCABULARY Numbers 2

a Read *An International Family*. Are the sentences true or false?

1 Pablo and Alicia have two small children.
2 María is married and lives in Turkey.
3 Pablo and Alicia live in Mexico.

An International Family

Pablo and Alicia Moreno are married. Pablo is from Spain, and Alicia is from Buenos Aires, in Argentina, but they live in New York. Their family is very international!

Alicia has a sister and a brother. Her sister, Daniela, is 46. She lives in Buenos Aires, and her mother lives there, too. Her brother, Carlos, is 37. He lives in Brazil, and he works in São Paulo.

Alicia and Pablo have two children. Their son, Alex, is 19. He's in college in Mexico, and he lives there, too. Their daughter, María, is 24. She lives in Istanbul with her Turkish husband, Mehmet.

4 GRAMMAR
Simple present: *he / she / it* affirmative

a Look at the verbs in the chart and answer the questions.

1 How are the verbs in A different from the verbs in B?
2 How is *has* different?

I / we / you / they	he / she / it
A	B
I **work** in an office.	He **works** in São Paulo.
We **have** two children.	She **has** a sister and a brother.
They **live** in New York.	She **lives** in Buenos Aires.

b Complete the sentences with verbs from 4a.

1 He _____ in an office.
2 He _____ at home with his parents.
3 Her mother _____ an apartment in New York.

c Now go to Grammar Focus 4B on p. 120.

d 💬🔊 **Communication 4B** Student A go to p. 105. Student B go to p. 109.

5 SPEAKING

a 💬🔊 Tell your partner about your family. Use the verbs in the box. Listen, but don't write notes.

have go study live work

My brother has two children – a boy and a girl.

b 💬🔊 Say what you remember about your partner's family. Are you correct?

35

Learn to ask and talk about photos

P Sound and spelling: /tʃ/ and /dʒ/

W Photo captions

Hector

Toby

1 LISTENING

a 💬 Ask and answer the questions.

1 Do you have photos of family and friends with you?
2 Where do you have them, on your phone or in your wallet?
3 How often do you look at them?

b ▶ 04.15 Listen to Part 1 and answer the questions.

1 Who writes Hector an email?
2 Where is he/she?

c ▶ 04.16 Listen to Part 2. Answer the questions.

1 How many people does Hector talk about?
2 How many people does Toby talk about?

d ▶ 04.16 Complete the information about Hector's and Toby's families with the words in the box. Then listen to Part 2 again and check your answers.

---
sister   cousin   teacher   hotel   computers   supermarket

Hector's mother's a ¹_____, and his father's the manager of a ²_____. He has a ³_____, Isa. Isa has two girls, Yasmin and Gabriela.
Toby has a brother, Mike. He works with ⁴_____ and is married to Kara. She's the manager of a ⁵_____. Troy also has a ⁶_____, James.

e 💬 Talk about a favorite photo of your family. Who's in it?

2 USEFUL LANGUAGE Asking and talking about photos

a Look at expressions 1–7 from Part 2. Do we use them to … ?

  a ask about photos
  b talk about your photos
  c talk about another person's photos

  1 This is my mother.
  2 Do you have photos of your family?
  3 Nice picture!
  4 Can I see them?
  5 Who's this?
  6 They're cute.
  7 This is my sister, Isa.

b ▶ 04.17 Look at expressions 1–4. Are they in group a, b, or c in 2a? Listen and check your answers in 2a and 2b.

  1 This is a picture of my town.
  2 It's really nice.
  3 Do you have any pictures of your home?
  4 These are my friends Rob and Mona.

c ▶ 04.18 **Pronunciation** Listen to the sentence. Answer the questions. Listen again and repeat.

This is my mother.

  1 Do the first two words connect?
  2 Is the pronunciation of *s* the same in *this* and *is*?

d ▶ 04.19 Complete the conversation with expressions in the box. Listen and check.

> Great photo!   Can I see them?
> He's funny.
> Do you have any photos of your friends?

  A ¹ _____
  B Yes, I do.
  A ² _____
  B Sure. This is a photo of my friend Marco.
  A ³ _____
  B And this is me with my friend Emilio.
  A Yes, I know Emilio. ⁴ _____
  B You're right – he's really funny.

e 💬 Practice the conversation in 2d. Take turns being A and B.

3 PRONUNCIATION Sound and spelling: /tʃ/ and /dʒ/

a ▶ 04.20 Listen and practice these sounds.

  1 /tʃ/ tea**ch**er pi**c**ture   2 /dʒ/ mana**g**er **J**ames

b ▶ 04.21 Listen to the words. Look at the sounds in **bold**. Which one is different in each group?

  1 **ch**ips **j**eans question
  2 lar**ge** **j**ob **ch**oose
  3 oran**ge** **ch**eap ma**tch**
  4 pa**ge** **ch**eese **G**ermany

c 💬 Practice saying the words in 3b.

4 SPEAKING

≫ **Communication 4C** Student A go to p. 105. Student B go to p. 108.

5 WRITING

a Read Hector's information about his sister. What information is new?

> 👤   This is my sister, Isa, with her two beautiful daughters, Yasmin and Gabriela. They live in a new house in Rio de Janeiro – it's very nice. Her husband, Pablo, isn't here, because it's his photo! They're a great family.

b ≫ Now go to Writing Plus 4C on p. 159 for Word order.

c Write about your photo from 1e. Here are some ideas:

  This is my … with …   He's / She's / They're …
  They live … It's nice / great!

d Read about your partner's photo. How many people does he/she write about?

✅ UNIT PROGRESS TEST

➡ **CHECK YOUR PROGRESS**

YOU CAN NOW DO THE UNIT PROGRESS TEST.

UNIT 4
Review

1 GRAMMAR

a Look at the words and write simple present questions.

> where / you / live   *Where do you live?*
1 what / your name
2 when / you / have lunch
3 what time / you / go to work
4 where / your friends / from
5 what / you / study
6 where / your school

b 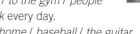 Ask and answer the questions in 1a.

c Correct the <u>underlined</u> words.

> My son <u>like</u> basketball. *likes*
1 Yolanda <u>work</u> in Boston.
2 Our daughter <u>eat</u> rice every day.
3 My city <u>haves</u> two universities.
4 Nacho <u>go</u> to school at 8:30.
5 My dad <u>teachs</u> Spanish.
6 My brother <u>studys</u> Chinese.

d <u>Underline</u> the correct answer.

1 When *are / 's / do* you work?
2 María *is live / live / lives* in Sydney.
3 Where *are / is / do* you from?
4 What *are / is / do* you have for breakfast?
5 What *are / is / do* their names?
6 What time do you *gos / go / goes* to school?

2 VOCABULARY

a Cross out the answer that is NOT possible.

> I work *in a factory / in an office / ~~tennis~~.*
1 I meet *my friends for coffee / to the gym / people at work* every day.
2 I play *home / baseball / the guitar.*
3 I live in *Italian / a small house / a big city.*
4 I teach *at a university / to the movies / young children.*
5 I study *English / in college / to school.*
6 I speak *Spanish / Japan / Chinese.*

b 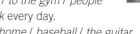 Which information in 2a is true for you? Tell a partner.

c Complete the numbers.

> 29 __twenty-__ nine
1 31 _____one
2 24 _____four
3 75 _____five
4 82 _____two
5 96 _____six
6 53 _____three
7 48 _____eight
8 67 _____seven
9 100 a _____

d Match 1–6 with the words in the box.

baby   boy   girl   men   woman   women

3 SOUND AND SPELLING

a ▶ 04.22 <u>Underline</u> ONE or TWO /ð/ sounds in each sentence. Practice saying the sentences.

1 These are my friends.
2 I study there.
3 This is my father.
4 They're at the movies.
5 They teach at the university.
6 She's their daughter.

b ▶ 04.23 Look at the information in the chart.

/tʃ/	/dʒ/
tea**ch**	mana**g**er
pi**c**ture	**g**ym
child	**J**ulia

c ▶ 04.24 Are the sounds in **bold** the same (S) or different (D)? Practice saying the sentences.

> We're on pa**g**e **s**eventy-two.   D
> He's a mana**g**er at the **g**ym.   S
1 **G**ary is a mana**g**er.
2 **J**ohn speaks **G**erman.
3 It's a pi**c**ture of the **g**ym.
4 She tea**ch**es the grammar on pa**g**e three.
5 It's a ques**t**ion about **ch**ildren.

🔄 CAN DO OBJECTIVES
- Describe a town
- Talk about hotels and hostels
- Ask about and say where places are

UNIT **5**

PLACES

GETTING STARTED

a 💬 Look at the picture and check (✓) the things you think are in the museum.

- [ ] art
- [ ] photos
- [ ] a restaurant
- [ ] a phone
- [ ] tickets
- [ ] a store

b 💬 Talk about the questions.

1 Who do you think visits this museum?
2 What other buildings do you think are near this museum?
3 Would you like to visit this museum?

5A | THERE ARE A FEW STORES

Learn to describe a town
G *there is / there are*: affirmative
V Places in a town

VERY HOT!

Stovepipe Wells, Death Valley, California

Stovepipe Wells is a small town in Death Valley in California. It's in the desert, so it's very dry, and it's also very hot during the day – it's sometimes 50°C in the summer. Only a few people live there, but there's a good road through the town, so there are a lot of tourists. In the town, there's a restaurant, there's a store, and there's a gas station. There are also two big hotels near the town. One of the hotels even has a golf course!

VERY COLD!

Resolute Bay, Canada

Resolute Bay is in the far north of Canada. It's cold in summer (4°C), and it's very cold in winter (–35°C). Also, because it's so far north, it's night from September to April. It's a very small place. Only about 200 people live there, but there's an airport, there are a few stores, there's a school for the children, and there are three small hotels. There are even a few cars, but there's only one good road in Resolute Bay. It goes from the town to the airport!

1 READING

a 💬 Look at the pictures of Resolute Bay and Stovepipe Wells. Which place is … ?

- in a desert
- on the ocean
- a good place for tourists

b Read about the two places and check your answers in 1a.

c Are the sentences about Resolute Bay (RB) or Stovepipe Wells (SW)?

1 "We often come here by car."
2 "It's always dark here in the winter."
3 "The school is small. There's only one teacher."
4 "There's a golf course at our hotel."
5 "Boats come here in the summer."

d 💬 Do you think Resolute Bay and Stovepipe Wells are … ?

- nice places to live?
- nice places for a vacation?

Why / Why not?

Language Plus *a few, a lot of*

a few cars   *a lot of* cars

a few stores   *a lot of* stores

2 GRAMMAR

there is / there are: affirmative

a Complete the sentences. Check your answers in the texts in 1b.

Singular: ¹_____ is a school / a good road.
Plural: There ²_____ three small hotels / a lot of tourists.

b ▶05.01 **Pronunciation** Listen and write the sentences. Tell the sentences to your partner.

c Now go to Grammar Focus 5A on p. 122.

d Cover the texts. Make sentences about the two places:

- hotels
- cars
- an airport
- stores
- schools

e 💬 Write two true sentences about your street. Use *there is* or *there are*. Check your partner's sentences.

3 VOCABULARY Places in a town

a ▶ 05.03 Match the words in the box with the places in pictures a–f. Listen and check.

café   store   restaurant
school   bank   hotel

b Which places in 3a are these?
1 "My daughter goes there every day."
2 "We go there for dinner every Saturday night."
3 "I often drink coffee there with my friends."
4 "You're in room 305. Here's your key."
5 "They have fruit and vegetables and also newspapers and magazines."
6 "I'd like $500, please."

c ≫ Now go to Vocabulary Focus 5A on p. 144.

d **Sound and spelling** /u/ and /ʌ/

1 ▶ 05.05 Listen and practice these sounds.
1 /u/ sch**oo**l   2 /ʌ/ l**u**nch

2 ▶ 05.06 Look at the words in the box. What sounds do the letters in **bold** have? Listen and add the words to the sound groups below.

s**u**mmer   f**oo**d   n**ew**   t**w**o   wh**o**   m**o**ther
umbrella   b**eau**tiful   s**o**metimes   p**oo**l

Sound 1 /u/	Sound 2 /ʌ/
school	lunch

3 💬 Practice saying the words.

4 LISTENING

a ▶ 05.07 Listen to a conversation about places in a town. Look at the map and match 1–5 with the words in the box.

bookstore   café   bank   restaurant   supermarket

b ▶ 05.07 Listen again. Are the sentences true or false?
1 There are a lot of stores on 14th Street.
2 Nice people work in the bookstore.
3 The café is Italian.
4 The coffee in the café isn't very good.
5 The restaurant on Main Street has Chinese food.
6 The restaurant is cheap.

c 💬 What is the same about the town on the map and your town?

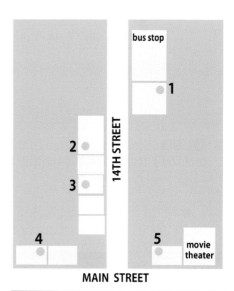

5 SPEAKING

a Think of a street in the town where you are now. Write notes. Use words from this lesson.
There's a …   There are …   It's in …   It's near …

b 💬 Describe your street, but don't say its name. Do other students know the name of the street?

IS THERE A HOSTEL IN YOUR TOWN?

1 VOCABULARY Hotels

a ▶05.08 Match the words in the box with pictures 1–5. Listen and check.

> bathtub   room   bed   TV   shower

b Sound and spelling /ʃ/

  1 ▶05.09 Listen and practice this sound.
  /ʃ/ **sh**ower

  2 ▶05.10 Listen to the words in the box. Underline the /ʃ/ sound in each word.

  > station   fish   sure   ocean

  3 💬 Practice saying the words.

c ⟫ Now go to Vocabulary Focus 5B on p. 138.

d ▶05.12 **Pronunciation** Listen to the words. Notice the stressed syllables. Practice saying them.

  hostel   hotel

e 💬 Which things in pictures 1–5 in 1a aren't in a hostel room?

hostel room

2 READING

a 💬 Look at pictures 1–3 of Turkey. Choose adjectives to talk about them. Compare your ideas with your partner.

- beautiful
- great
- nice
- boring
- exciting
- interesting
- old
- big

b Read Sandra's review of a hostel in Turkey. Does Sandra like the hostel?

c Read the review again. Check (✓) what's in the hostel.

third floor	☐ small rooms	☐ big rooms	☐ café
second floor	☐ restaurant	☐ TV room	☐ small rooms
first floor	☐ café	☐ kitchen	☐ TV room

d 💬 Would you like to stay at the hostel? Why / Why not?

HOSTEL REVIEWS

The Cave Hostel ★★★★★

This is a great hostel in Göreme, in Turkey. It's in Cappadocia, a very old part of the country. You can do a lot of things here. My favorite thing is going in a hot air balloon. You can see really beautiful places from the air.

The hostel has different rooms with different prices. On the second floor, there are small rooms for two people with bathtubs. On the third floor, there are big rooms with six beds in them. They're very cheap, but there isn't a shower or a bathtub in the big rooms. There aren't any blankets or pillows – you pay for those. There isn't a restaurant or café in the hostel, but there's a kitchen on the first floor. There aren't any TVs in the rooms, but there's free Wi-Fi. It's a very simple place to stay, and it's clean. And the people are very friendly. Faruk, the manager, sings karaoke really well!
Sandra

3 GRAMMAR *there is / there are*: negative

a ▶ 05.13 Complete the sentences with *isn't* or *aren't*. Listen and check.

1 There _____ any blankets.
2 There _____ a restaurant.

b Find more examples of *there isn't* and *there aren't* in Sandra's review.

c Think about the town or city you're in now. Check (✓) the sentences that are true. Correct the false sentences.

1 ☐ There's a big museum in this town / city.
2 ☐ There are a lot of stores here.
3 ☐ There aren't any hostels.
4 ☐ There are two bus stations.
5 ☐ There aren't any parks.

d 💬🔊 Read your sentences and listen to your partner's sentences. Are they the same?

> There aren't any museums in this town.

> Yes, there is a museum in this town – on Cromwell Road.

4 LISTENING

a ▶ 05.14 Listen to a hostel receptionist and George, a guest. Is George happy with the hostel?

b ▶ 05.14 Listen again. Check (✓) the things in the hostel.

☐ available rooms ☐ café ☐ Wi-Fi
☐ parking ☐ kitchen ☐ showers

c 💬🔊 Why do people like hostels? Why do people like hotels?

5 GRAMMAR *there is / there are*: questions

a ▶ 05.15 Complete the questions. Listen and check.

1 Singular: _____ _____ a restaurant here?
   Yes, there's a restaurant here.
2 Plural: _____ _____ any cafés near here?
   Yes, there are cafés near here.

b 💬🔊 Now go to Grammar Focus 5B on p. 122.

c Write questions using *Is there … ?* and *Are there … ?* about your partner's town, city, or street. Here are some ideas:

- cafés
- swimming pool
- movie theater
- supermarket
- hospital
- restaurants

d 💬🔊 Ask your partner about their town, city, or street.

> Are there any cafés in your town?

> Yes, there are two cafés.

> Is there a supermarket on your street?

> No, but there are two stores.

6 SPEAKING

≫ **Communication 5B**
Student A go to p. 109.
Student B go to p. 107.

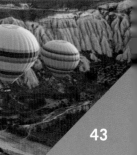

5C EVERYDAY ENGLISH
Is there a café near here?

Learn to ask about and say where places are
P Emphasizing what you say 1
W An email about a place

1 LISTENING

a 💬🔊 Ask and answer the questions.

1 What stores or supermarkets are there near your home?
2 Do you go to these stores or supermarkets? How often?
3 Is the food good / expensive?

b ▶️ 05.18 Listen to Part 1. Answer the questions.

1 Does Anya like the hotel room?
2 What do Anya and Lily want to drink?
3 Do they know the area near their hotel?

2 PRONUNCIATION Emphasizing what you say 1

a ▶️ 05.19 Listen to the sentence.

ANYA It's really small, but it's OK.

▶️ 05.20 Listen to the sentence again. Is *really* more or less stressed the second time?

b Check (✓) the correct rule.

We say *really* with a strong stress to:
1 ☐ speak loudly
2 ☐ make the meaning stronger

c ▶️ 05.21 Listen to the sentences. <u>Underline</u> one word with strong stress in each sentence.

1 My country is very hot in the summer.
2 James's new car is really fast.
3 This movie is so boring.

d ▶️ 05.21 Listen again and repeat.

3 LISTENING

a ▶️ 05.22 Listen to Part 2. Answer the questions.

1 Do Lily and Anya find a café near their hotel?
2 Who do they see on the street?

b ▶️ 05.22 Listen to Part 2 again. Are the sentences true or false?

1 Lily thinks a store is a café.
2 Sebastien sees Lily and Anya first.
3 Sebastien works in Paris.
4 There's a café near their hotel.
5 There's a café near Sebastien's apartment.

4 USEFUL LANGUAGE Asking and saying where places are

a ▶ 05.23 Complete the questions with words in the box. Listen and check.

near   where   there

1 _____'s our hotel?
2 Is _____ a supermarket near here?
3 Are there any stores _____ here?

b ▶ 05.24 Match the two possible answers in a–c with questions 1–3 in 4a. Listen and check.

a Yes, there are. There's one on this street. / No, sorry, there aren't.
b Yes, there's one near the bank. / No, sorry, there isn't.
c It's on the next street. / It's on this street.

c ▶ 05.25 Put the conversation in the correct order. Listen and check.

A ☐ Great, thank you. And is there a good restaurant in this part of town?
A ☐1 Excuse me, can you help me?
A ☐ OK, thanks for your help.
A ☐ Are there any good cafés near here?
B ☐ Yes, there's one on the next street – Park Café.
B ☐ No, I'm sorry, there are no restaurants near here. But there's one near the bus station.
B ☐ Yes, of course.
B ☐ No problem.

d 💬 Practice the conversation in 4c with a partner.

5 SPEAKING

≫ **Communication 5C** Student A look at the information below. Student B go to p. 106.

a Conversation 1. You're on a street you don't know. Ask Student B about:
• a hotel   • cafés

b Conversation 2. Now you're on a street you know. Use the information to answer Student B's questions.
• a bank: on the next street
• stores: not near here – near the hospital

6 WRITING

a Read part of an email from Lily to her parents. She writes about her trip to Paris. Does she only write about the good things?

● ● ●

Paris is great! Our hotel is in a nice part of the city, but it's really small. There's a beautiful park near the hotel, and there are stores on the next street. And guess what! I'm at a café with Sebastien! He is really good! His apartment is nice, but it's not near our hotel.

...

b ≫ Go to Writing Plus 5C on p. 160 for *and* and *but*.

c Write about your part of town. Use *there's / there isn't / there are / there aren't*. Use *and* and *but*.

d Read about your partner's part of town. Is it the same?

✓ UNIT PROGRESS TEST

→ **CHECK YOUR PROGRESS**

YOU CAN NOW DO THE UNIT PROGRESS TEST.

UNIT 5
Review

1 GRAMMAR

a Correct the sentences.

> There an Italian restaurant.   *There's an Italian restaurant.*
1 There is a hotel on this street?
2 Yes, there's.
3 There are a shower.
4 There aren't a available rooms.
5 Is there swimming pool at the hotel?
6 No, there not is.

b Complete the sentences.

1 Is _____ a bank near here?
2 Are there _____ bottles of water in the room?
3 _____ there a supermarket on this street?
4 Is there _____ TV in the room?
5 _____ there any cafés near here?
6 Is there _____ teacher in the room?

c 💬 Ask and answer the questions in 1b.

2 VOCABULARY

a What are these places? Use the words to complete the crossword.

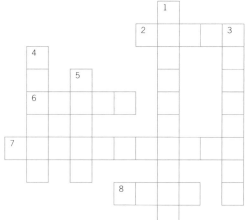

b Write the words.

1 d e b _____   5 o r o m _____

2 w e r h o s _____   6 w o t e l _____

3 i p o w l l _____   7 i W-i F _____

4 t h t a u b b _____   8 k a n b l e t _____

3 SOUND AND SPELLING

a ▶ 05.26 Complete the chart with the words in the box. Practice saying the words.

up   you   umbrella   lunch   summer   beautiful   new
brother   school   mother   food   pool

/u/	/ʌ/
you	up

b ▶ 05.27 Look at the information in the chart.

/ɑ/	/aʊ/	/oʊ/
lot	shower	pillow
hospital	flower	know
hot	towel	hotel

c ▶ 05.28 Are the sounds in **bold** the same (S) or different (D)? Practice saying the words.

> t**ow**n – a l**o**t D
1 h**o**t – h**o**tel   4 g**o** – pill**ow**
2 sh**ow**er – h**ow**   5 h**o**t – t**ow**el
3 **O**K – kn**ow**   6 fl**ow**er – h**o**spital

⟳ CAN DO OBJECTIVES

- Talk about people's jobs
- Talk about daily routines and habits
- Make and accept offers

UNIT **6**

WORK AND ROUTINES

GETTING STARTED

a 💬 Look at the picture and answer the questions.

1 What do the people do?
2 Where do the people work?
3 Would you like to do this job?

b 💬 Think of two questions to ask the people in the picture.

⚙ JOBS INTERNATIONAL

HOME   NEWS   ABOUT

HELP AROUND THE WORLD ...

Welcome to Jobs International. Our people go around the world and help others. Meet two of them.

I'm a doctor from Brazil, and I work in a small hospital in Ghana. I love the work here because it's very interesting. I do different things every day. And the people are so friendly. Life isn't always easy here, but it's great to help people.

LUIZA

I'm a teacher at a school in Samoa, but I'm from Australia. I teach English here and after school, I play sports with the children. They love rugby and volleyball. The children are really happy – a lot of fun. This is a really good job.

FRED

1 READING

a 💬 Look at pictures a and b. What places are in the pictures? What jobs do people do there?

b Read about Luiza and Fred on the *Jobs International* website. Are your ideas in 1a correct?

c Read the website again. Are the sentences true or false?

1 *Jobs International* people don't work in their home countries.
2 Luiza works in a big hospital.
3 Her work is sometimes boring.
4 She likes the people in Ghana.
5 Fred goes home after classes.
6 His students like playing sports.

d Write questions for Luiza and Fred.
What ... do? → *What do you do?*

1 Where ... work?
2 ... like the people?
3 ... like the job?

e 💬 You are Luiza or Fred. Ask and answer the questions in 1d.

What do you do?

I'm a teacher.

Language Plus *work / job*

*I **work** in a hospital.*	*work* = verb
*I like my **work**.*	*work* = noun
*It's a good **job**.*	*job* = noun (*doctor, teacher*)

2 LISTENING AND VOCABULARY Jobs

a Match the words in the box with pictures a–h.

| soccer player | student | receptionist | server | taxi driver | factory worker | office worker | sales assistant |

b ▶ 06.01 **Pronunciation** Listen to the two-word jobs in 2a. Which word is stressed?

1 the first word
2 the second word

💬🔊 Practice saying the words.

c ▶ 06.02 Listen to four people talk about their jobs. What do they do?

1 _____   3 _____
2 _____   4 _____

d ▶ 06.02 Listen again. Complete the sentences with the words in the box.

| study | play (x2) | sit | meet (x2) |

1 **ANNA** I _____ all day, but I _____ some interesting people and go to a lot of different places. I don't work at night.
2 **FELIPE** I _____ on a team, and the weekend is the most important time of the week in my job. I don't _____ games during the week – well, sometimes on Wednesdays.
3 **MARIA** I _____ business at college. It's really interesting.
4 **JESSICA** I work in a store and _____ a lot of different people.

e 💬🔊 Which job do you like in 2c? Which job don't you like? Say why.

f ≫ Now go to Vocabulary Focus 6A on p. 145.

3 GRAMMAR Simple present: *he / she / it* negative

a ▶ 06.04 Complete the sentences with *does* or *doesn't*. Listen and check.

ANNA I don't work at night.
1 She _____ work at night.
FELIPE I don't play games during the week.
2 He _____ play games during the week.

b ≫ Now go to Grammar Focus 6A on p. 124.

c Complete the sentences with the correct form of the verbs in parentheses.

1 Alex is a taxi driver. He _____ in the morning. (not work)
2 Sam is a bank teller. He _____ his job. (not like)
3 Lucy is a sales assistant. She _____ much during the day. (not sit)
4 Matteo is a server. He _____ on Monday. (not work)

d Sound and spelling /ʃ/ and /tʃ/

1 ▶ 06.06 Listen to the words. Do the letters in **bold** have the same sound?
she   **ch**ildren   recep**ti**onist   tea**ch**

2 ▶ 06.07 Listen to the words in the box. Which words have **sound 1 /ʃ/** and which have **sound 2 /tʃ/**?

| **sh**ort | **ch**eap | wa**tch** | fini**sh** | **st**ation | kit**ch**en |

3 Which two letters often make sound 2?

4 💬🔊 Practice saying the words in 2.

4 SPEAKING

≫ **Communication 6A** Student A go to p. 109. Student B go to p. 107.

6B | I WAKE UP AT 4:00

A Good Night's Sleep

People say it's good to sleep for eight hours every night … but is it true? Some people sleep for only five or six hours, and they feel fine in the morning. And some people sleep twice every night …

Anneli Hanka, 24, Finland

I always **wake up** at about 4:00 in the morning. I don't want to sleep, so I **get up**, and I do yoga. Then I **go to bed** again. Then I get up at 8:00 in the morning, and I go to work. I feel fine – I never feel tired.

Beatriz Romero, 32, U.S.

I finish work at 6:00 in the evening, and I arrive home at 6:30. I read the news or text a friend. Then I go to bed for three hours. My husband works at a restaurant, and he gets home at about 12:00 at night. So I get up, we have dinner, and then we watch TV until about 3:00. Then I sleep until 7:00.

1 READING AND VOCABULARY Daily routine

a Talk about when you do these things. Use the phrases in the box.

in the morning	in the afternoon	in the evening	at night

1 have dinner
2 go to English class
3 work
4 have coffee
5 read the news
6 sleep

b Read the text above. Match what Beatriz and Anneli say with pictures a and b.

c Match the underlined words from the text with pictures 1–3.

d Complete the verb phrases with the words in the box. Then read the text again to check your answers.

have	watch	go	arrive / get	finish

1 _____ to work
2 _____ home
3 _____ dinner
4 _____ TV
5 _____ work

e ≫ Now go to Vocabulary Focus 6B on p. 146.

f Ask and answer the questions with a partner.

1 Do you sleep … ?
  • for eight hours
  • twice every night
  • for five or six hours
2 When do you usually … ?
  • wake up • get up • go to bed
3 When do you usually … ?
  • go to work or school • finish work or school
  • get home in the evening

Language Plus *for, from … to … , until*

← 8 hours →
11:00 p.m.	7:00 a.m.

*I sleep **for** eight hours.*
*I sleep **from** 11:00 **to** 7:00.*
*I sleep **until** 7:00.*

g **Sound and spelling** Consonant clusters

1 ▶ 06.10 These words start with two consonant sounds together. Listen and practice saying them.
sleep **br**eakfast **tw**elve

2 ▶ 06.11 Listen to the words in the box. Underline the two consonant sounds that are together.

play	small	bread	fruit	driver	study	speak

3 Practice saying the words.

2 LISTENING

a ▶ 06.12 Listen to an interview with Paul. What are his answers to the questions?

1 Do you go to bed early?
2 When do you wake up?
3 What do you do then?
4 What about your wife? Does she wake up then?

b 💬 Talk about the questions with a partner.

1 What do you think about Paul's daily routine?
2 What do you think about his photos? Think of adjectives to talk about them.

3 GRAMMAR Simple present: *he / she / it* questions

a Complete the questions in the chart with *do* or *does*.

you	he/she/it
___Do___ you go to bed early?	_____ she wake up?
When _____ you wake up?	When _____ he get up?

b ≫ Now go to Grammar Focus 6B on p. 124.

c ▶ 06.15 Pronunciation Listen to the questions with *when* in 3a and notice the stressed words. Check (✓) the words we stress.

1 ☐ question word (*when*)
2 ☐ *do*
3 ☐ *up*

d Write questions about Beatriz and Anneli on page 50.

1 What time / Beatriz / finish work?
2 Where / her husband / work?
3 What time / he / get home?
4 When / Anneli / wake up?
5 What / she / do then?
6 How / she / feel in the morning?

e 💬 Ask and answer the questions in 3d with a partner.

I take photos at night.

Paul

f 💬 Ask about your partner's routine.

- the morning
- meals
- work / school / college
- the evening
- sleep

When do you get up?

I get up at 7:30.

g 💬 Work with a new partner. Ask questions about their first partner's routine.

When does Emma get up?

Emma gets up at 7:30.

4 SPEAKING

≫ Communication 6B Student A go to p. 109. Student B go to p. 107.

6C | EVERYDAY ENGLISH
I'll come with you

Learn to make and accept offers
P Emphasizing what you say 2
W An email about your day

1 LISTENING

a You want to have a birthday party for your friend. Check (✓) four things you need.

1 ☐ a cake   4 ☐ ice cream
2 ☐ pizza   5 ☐ soda
3 ☐ cups   6 ☐ plates

b 💬🗩 Tell a partner your ideas in 1a. Do you need the same things?

c ▶06.16 Listen to Part 1. Answer the questions.

1 Who does Zoey see on the street?
2 When does Ariana want to go shopping?

d ▶06.16 Listen to Part 1 again. Underline the correct word.

1 The flowers are for *Zoey* / *Ariana*.
2 *Zoey* / *Evan* wants coffee.
3 *Ariana* / *Zoey* loves to cook.
4 Ariana *wants* / *doesn't want* a birthday party.

2 USEFUL LANGUAGE   Making and accepting offers 1

a ▶06.17 Complete the conversation with the words in the box. Listen and check.

thanks   please   like

ARIANA   Would you _____ some coffee?
EVAN   No, that's OK, _____.
ZOEY   Yes, _____!

b ▶06.17 **Pronunciation** Listen to the mini-conversation in 2a again. What sounds do *would* and *you* make together? Listen again and repeat.

c ▶06.18 Put A's questions in the correct order in the conversation. Listen and check.

A like / would you / some coffee ?
B Yes, please.
A piece of cake / you like a / and would ?
B No, that's OK, thanks.

d 💬🗩 Practice the conversation in 2c with a partner. Ask about different food and drinks.

Would you like a glass of orange juice?

Yes, please.

Would you like a sandwich?

No, thanks.

3 LISTENING AND USEFUL LANGUAGE
Making and accepting offers 2

a ▶ 06.19 Listen to Part 2. Answer the questions.
1 What does Evan want to do?
2 Do Ariana and Zoey accept his help?

b ▶ 06.20 Complete the sentences with words in the box. Listen and check.

| can | help | I'll |

1 I _____ go with you.
2 I'll _____ you buy things.
3 _____ come with you.

c ▶ 06.21 Do these replies answer yes or no? Listen and check.

That's great, thanks.   Don't worry, that's OK.
Thanks, but I'm fine.   Thank you, that's very nice of you.

d ▶ 06.22 Complete the conversation with the words in the box. Listen and check.

| great | can | help | right | supermarket |

A I need to go to the ¹_____.
B I ²_____ come with you.
A That's ³_____! And I need to make dinner.
B I'll ⁴_____ you.
A All ⁵_____, thank you so much.

e Practice the conversation in 3d with a partner.

f Use different words and expressions to make a new conversation.

I need to go shopping.

I'll go with you.

4 PRONUNCIATION
Emphasizing what you say 2

a ▶ 06.23 Listen to the sentences and notice the strong stress. Then listen again and repeat.
1 I can go with you.   2 I'll come with you.

b ▶ 06.24 Listen to the mini-conversations. Underline the strong stress.
Conversation 1
A I can't do this exercise.
B José can help you.
Conversation 2
C I need to get to the bus station this afternoon.
D I'll drive you.

c Practice the mini-conversations in 4b with a partner.

5 SPEAKING

a You're at a café with your partner. Use the ideas below to make a conversation.

6 WRITING

a Read part of an email from Ariana to her sister. She writes about a day in her life in Los Angeles. Where do Ariana and Zoey have coffee? Why?

● ● ●

I walk to work every day because my apartment is near the office. I start work at 8:30, and I finish at 5:30. I work with Zoey. We go out to a café for coffee every day because the coffee machine in the office isn't very good. We also have lunch there. They have great pizza and chocolate cake – my favorite! Zoey always says, "I'll pay." She's really nice.

b Now go to Writing Plus 6C on p. 160 for *because* and *also*.

c Write about a day in your life. Use *because* and *also*.

d Read about your partner's day. Do you do the same?

UNIT PROGRESS TEST

→ CHECK YOUR PROGRESS

YOU CAN NOW DO THE UNIT PROGRESS TEST.

UNIT 6
Review

1 GRAMMAR

a Check (✓) the sentences that are correct. Correct the mistakes.

> My sister doesn't lives at home.
> *My sister doesn't live at home.*
> ✓ I don't study Chinese.
1 ☐ She don't like cake.
2 ☐ Marcus doesn't meets many people.
3 ☐ This town doesn't have a university.
4 ☐ I work not on Fridays.
5 ☐ We don't talk much at work.
6 ☐ Isabella speaks not Italian.

b Complete the sentences with *do*, *don't*, *does*, or *doesn't*.

1 _____ your sister work in a bank?
No, she 2 _____.

3 _____ you meet people at work?
Yes, I 4 _____.

5 _____ you and your friends play basketball?
No, we 6 _____.

c Write simple present questions with the words and phrases.

> what time / you / get up
> *What time do you get up?*
1 what / you / eat in the morning
2 where / your brother / work
3 you / speak / English
4 your teacher / speak / Spanish
5 what time / the class / start
6 when / it / end

d 💬 Ask and answer the questions in 1c.

2 VOCABULARY

a Complete the job words.

1 s_____r   2 t___id____r   3 d_____r

4 r_____t   5 t_____r   6 c_____f

b Complete the chart with the words and phrases in the box.

arrive   get   start   to bed   lunch
shower   ~~to school~~   take

go	_to school_ / to work
	1 _____
wake 2 _____	up
3 _____ finish	work
have	breakfast / 4 _____ / dinner a coffee
5 _____ / get	home
6 _____	a shower

c 💬 What do you do every day? Tell a partner.

3 SOUND AND SPELLING

a ▶06.25 Listen to the sounds in **bold** and put the words in the correct box.

chair   information   spe**ci**al   **ch**icken   **ch**eck   ma**ch**ine

/ʃ/	/tʃ/

b ▶06.26 Look at the pair of words. Put the words in the box into similar pairs.

sound 1 /ʃ/   sound 2 /tʃ/
ship   –   **ch**ip

choose   cash   wash   cheap   cheese
watch   sheep   catch   she's   shoes

c ▶06.27 Match the words that start with the same consonant group. Practice saying the words.

bread   class   ~~drink~~   player   sport   start   twenty

> **dr**iver – ___drink___
1 **tw**elve – _____
2 **st**udy – _____
3 **pl**ate – _____
4 **cl**ock – _____
5 **br**eakfast – _____
6 **sp**oon – _____

🔄 REVIEW YOUR PROGRESS

How well did you do in this unit? Write 3, 2, or 1 for each objective.
3 = very well   2 = well   1 = not so well

I CAN ...	
talk about people's jobs	☐
talk about daily routines and habits	☐
make and accept offers	☐

Phonemic symbols

Vowel sounds

/ə/	/æ/	/ʊ/	/ɑ/	/ɪ/	/i/	/e/	/ʌ/	/ɜ/	/u/	/ɔ/
breakf**a**st	m**a**n	p**u**t	g**o**t	ch**i**p	happ**y**	m**e**n	**u**p	sh**ir**t	wh**o**	w**a**lk

Diphthongs (two vowel sounds)

/eə/	/ɪə/	/ɔɪ/	/ɑɪ/	/eɪ/	/oʊ/	/ɑʊ/
h**air**	n**ear**	b**oy**	n**i**ne	**ei**ght	wind**ow**	n**ow**

Consonants

/p/	/b/	/f/	/v/	/t/	/d/	/k/	/g/
picnic	**b**ook	**f**ace	**v**ery	**t**ime	**d**og	**c**old	**g**o
/θ/	/ð/	/tʃ/	/dʒ/	/s/	/z/	/ʃ/	/ʒ/
think	**th**e	**ch**air	**j**ob	**s**ea	**z**oo	**sh**oe	televi**si**on
/m/	/n/	/ŋ/	/h/	/l/	/r/	/w/	/j/
me	**n**ow	si**ng**	**h**ot	**l**ate	**r**ed	**w**ent	**y**es

Irregular verbs

Infinitive	Simple past
be	was
begin	began
buy	bought
catch	caught
choose	chose
come	came
do	did
drink	drank
drive	drove
eat	ate
feel	felt
find	found
fly	flew
forget	forgot
get	got
give	gave
go	went
grow up	grew up
have	had
hear	heard
know	knew
leave	left
lose	lost

Infinitive	Simple past
meet	met
pay	paid
put	put
read	read
ride	rode
run	ran
say	said
see	saw
sell	sold
send	sent
sing	sang
sit	sat
sleep	slept
speak	spoke
swim	swam
take	took
teach	taught
tell	told
think	thought
understand	understood
wake up	woke up
wear	wore
write	wrote

COMMUNICATION PLUS

1A STUDENT A

a You're Yoshi from Japan. You're a student. Complete the conversation.

  A Hello, I'm _____.
  B Hi, I'm Bella. Nice to meet you.
  A Are you from the U.K.?
  B No, I'm not. I'm from the U.S. And you?
  A I'm from _____.
  B Are you a teacher?
  A No, I'm a _____. And you?
  B I'm a teacher.

b Have a conversation with Student B.

c Choose a name and a country and have another conversation.

1B STUDENT A

Jenna = British   Diego = Ecuadorian   Sandra = Italian

a Look at the picture and the information box. Then cover the box.

b Tell Student B the names of the people and answer Student B's questions.

This is ...

c Listen to Student B talk about the people in the picture. Then ask Student B about the nationalities of the people.

Are they Spanish?

No, they're not. They're Brazilian.

2A STUDENT A

a Read the information about Kate.
  Name: Kate
  Town/city: Beaverton – small city near Portland, Oregon, in the U.S.
  Home: beautiful, old house

b Tell Students B and C about Kate.

  Her name's ...

  She's from ...

  Her home is ...

c Listen to Students B and C talk about two people. What information is the same about all three people?

2B STUDENT A

a Look at the picture. Student B has a similar picture. Ask and answer questions to find seven differences.

Do you have a phone in your picture?

I have two phones.

b ≫ Now go back to p. 19.

4C STUDENT A

a Look at the pictures. The two people are your friends. You want to show the pictures to Student B. Think about what you want to say.

Rob, teacher, interesting

Carla, hotel manager, happy

b Cover the information under the pictures. Show them to Student B and talk about your friends.

These are my friends Rob and Carla.

c Ask Student B about his/her two friends.

Do you have photos of your friends?

d ≫ Now go back to p. 37.

4A STUDENT A

a Read the information.

• You live in Montreal, Canada, but you work three days a week in Essex, Vermont, in the U.S.
• You work two days a week from home.
• You study French and you go to class on Friday.

b Start a conversation with Student B about their life. Use the questions below to help you.

Where do you live?

Do you work in …?

Do you speak …?

c Listen to Student B and reply.

I live in …   *I speak a little …*

2C STUDENT A

a Ask Student B about his/her:

• last name
• address
• phone number
• email address

What's your last name?

b Read the information on your card. Answer Student B's questions.

> **Last name:** Ramirez
> **Address:** 5 High Street
> **Phone number:** (714) 555-4321
> **Email address:** toniramirez@travelmail.com

c ≫ Now go back to p. 20.

3B STUDENT A

a Ask Student B the time in these cities:

• Paris
• Rio de Janeiro
• Beijing
• Los Angeles

b Answer Student B's questions about the time in these cities.

Tokyo   New York   Mexico City   Berlin

c ≫ Now go back to p. 27.

4B STUDENT A

a Read the information about Omar on your card.

"I'm a student. I'm 19, and I study English at Cairo University, in Egypt. I live at home with my parents. My mother is a teacher, and my father works at the Bank of Cairo. He's a bank manager. I have one brother. He's married, and he lives in Dubai. He works at Dubai Airport."

b Tell Student B about Omar.

He's a student. He studies English …

c Listen to Student B talk about Monica. Find six things that are the same about Omar and Monica.

1 They're both students.

d ≫ Now go back to p. 35.

1A STUDENT B

a You're Bella from the U.S. You're a teacher. Complete the conversation.

   A Hello, I'm Yoshi.
   B Hi, I'm _____. Nice to meet you.
   A Are you from England?
   B No, I'm not. I'm from _____. And you?
   A I'm from Japan.
   B Are you a _____?
   A No, I'm a student. And you?
   B I'm a _____.

b Have a conversation with Student A.

c Choose a name and a country and have another conversation.

1B STUDENT B

Sara = Spanish   Luis and Marta = Brazilian   Tony = American

a Look at the picture and the information in the box. Then cover the box.

b Listen to Student A talk about the people in the picture. Then ask Student A about the nationalities of the people.

   Is he British?

          No, he's not. He's American.

c Tell Student A the names of the people and answer Student A's questions.

          This is …

2A STUDENT B

a Read the information about Carla.

   Name: Carla
   Town/city: Hamilton – small city near Toronto, in Canada
   Home: nice, new apartment

b Listen to Student A.

c Tell Students A and C about Carla.

   Her name's …

          She's from …

              Her home is …

d Listen to Student C talk. What information is the same about all three people?

2B STUDENT B

a Look at the picture. Student A has a similar picture. Ask and answer questions to find seven differences.

   Do you have keys
   in your picture?

          I have one key.

b ≫ Now go back to p. 19.

5C STUDENT B

a **Conversation 1.** You're on a street you know. Use the information to answer Student A's questions.

   a hotel: not near here – near the train station
   cafés: Black Cat Café on this street

b **Conversation 2.** Now you're on a street you don't know. Ask Student A about:

   • a bank • stores

c ≫ Now go back to p. 45.

5B STUDENT B

a Read the information about a hotel on your card.

Hotel Helena

- Rooms with showers and TVs
- Restaurant
- Swimming pool
- Parking

Note: *There isn't free Wi-Fi in the hotel.*
You pay for it.

b Student A has information about a hostel. Ask and answer questions to find what things are the same and what things are different in the hotel and the hostel.

Is there free Wi-Fi in the hostel?

Yes, there is.

6A STUDENT B

a Look at the information about Sarah and Hassan. Make affirmative (+) and negative (−) sentences.

+ meet a lot of people   − work in the morning
+ work in a restaurant   − sit a lot
→ a server

Sarah

+ meet a lot of people   − work during the day
+ like his job   − work very hard
→ a taxi driver

Hassan

b Ask Student A about Rosa and Franco.
Say: *Tell me about ... .*
Can you guess their jobs?

Rosa   Franco

c Tell Student A about Sarah and Hassan. Don't say their jobs.

Sarah meets a lot of people.

3B STUDENT B

a Answer Student A's questions about the time in these cities.

Paris   Rio de Janeiro   Beijing   Los Angeles

b Ask Student A the time in these cities:
- Tokyo
- New York
- Mexico City
- Berlin

c ≫ Now go back to p. 27.

6B STUDENT B

a Peter and Gamal live in the same apartment. Read about Peter's daily routine.

Peter works at a bank. He always wakes up at 6:30. He gets up at 7:00, has coffee, and goes to work. He starts work at 8:30, and he finishes at 5:30. He gets home at 6:00, has dinner, and watches TV. Sometimes he goes out, but he always goes to bed at 10:30.

Peter

b Answer Student A's questions about Peter.

c Ask Student A questions about Gamal. Then write the answers.

When does he go to class?

What does he do in the afternoon?

- When / get up? *9:00*
- When / go to class?
- What / do in the afternoon?
- When / get home?
- What / do in the evening?
- When / start work?
- When / finish work?
- When / go to bed?

d When does Peter see Gamal?

4A STUDENT B

a Read the information.

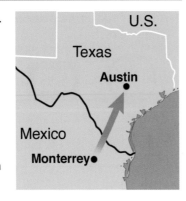

- You live in Monterrey, Mexico, but you work four days a week in Austin, Texas, in the U.S.
- You work one day a week from home.
- You study Spanish and you go to class on Saturday.

b Listen to Student A and reply.

I live in …

I speak a little …

c Start a conversation with Student A about their life. Use the questions below to help you.

Where do you live?

Do you work in …?

Do you speak …?

4C STUDENT B

a Look at the pictures. The two people are your friends. You want to show the pictures to Student A. Think about what you want to say.

Haley, student, kind

Will, bank manager, funny

b Ask Student A about his/her two friends.

Do you have photos of your friends?

c Cover the information under the pictures. Show them to Student A and talk about your friends.

These are my friends Haley and Will.

d ≫ Now go back to p. 37.

2A STUDENT C

a Read the information about Dave.

Name: Dave
Town/city: Newcastle – small city near Sydney, in Australia
Home: big, new apartment

b Listen to Students A and B talk about two people.

c Tell Students A and B about Dave. What information is the same about all three people?

His name's …

He's from …

His home is …

2C STUDENT B

a Read the information on your card. Answer Student A's questions.

Last name: Adams
Address: 8 Park Road
Phone number: (714) 555-9876
Email address: alexadams@travelmail.com

b Ask Student A about his/her:

- last name
- address
- phone number
- email address

What's your last name?

c ≫ Now go back to p. 20.

4B STUDENT B

a Read the information about Monica on your card.

"I'm Peruvian. I'm 20. I live in Lima, and I study English in college. I live at home with my parents. I have a brother and two sisters. My brother works at the airport. He's married and he has two children."

b Listen to Student A talk about Omar.

c Tell Student A about Monica. Find six things that are the same about Omar and Monica.

> She's a student.
> She studies English ...

> *1 They're both students.*

d ≫ Now go back to p. 35.

5B STUDENT A

a Read the information about a hostel on your card.

HARRY'S HOSTEL

- Big rooms with no shower
- Small rooms with a shower
- Free Wi-Fi
- A small café

Note: There isn't a swimming pool or parking.

b Student B has information about a hotel. Ask and answer questions to find what things are the same and what things are different in the hotel and the hostel.

> Is there a swimming pool in the hotel?

> Yes, there is.

6B STUDENT A

a Gamal and Peter live in the same apartment. Read about Gamal's daily routine.

Gamal is a student. He usually gets up at 9:00 and has breakfast. Then he goes to class at 10:00. In the afternoon, he studies in the library, and he gets home at 5:00. In the evening, he works in a café near their apartment. He starts work at 7:00 and finishes at 11:00. He goes to bed at 12:00.

b Ask Student B questions about Peter. Then write the answers.

> When does he get up?

> What does he do then?

- When / wake up? *6:30*
- When / get up?
- What / do then?
- When / start work?

- When / finish work?
- When / get home?
- What / do in the evening?
- When / go to bed?

c Answer Student B's questions about Gamal.

d When does Gamal see Peter?

6A STUDENT A

a Look at the information about Rosa and Franco. Make affirmative (+) and negative (–) sentences.

- + work very hard
- + work at a hospital
- → a doctor

- – have a lot of free time
- – sit a lot

- + work long hours
- + like his job
- → a teacher

- – sit a lot
- – work in the summer

b Tell Student B about Rosa and Franco. Don't say their jobs.

> Rosa works very hard.

c Ask Student B about Sarah and Hassan. Say: *Tell me about ... .* Can you guess their jobs?

GRAMMAR FOCUS

1A *be*: *I / you / we*

Part 1: Affirmative and questions
▶ 01.03

	Affirmative (+)
I	*I'm fine.*
you	*You're right.*
we	*We're from the U.S.*
you	*You're John and Hannah.*

> 💭 **Tip**
> I am → I'm
> You are → You're
> We are → We're

▶ 01.05

	Wh- questions (?)
I	*Where am I?*
you	*How are you?*
we	*Where are we?*
you	*Where are you?*

▶ 01.04

Yes/No questions (?)		Short answers	
Am I	at home?	Yes, you **are**.	No, you**'re not**.
Are you	OK?	Yes, I **am**.	No, I**'m not**.
Are we	in Los Angeles?	Yes, you **are**.	No, you**'re not**.
Are you	students?	Yes, we **are**.	No, we**'re not**.

Are you from Spain? NOT ~~You are from Spain?~~
Yes, **I am**. NOT ~~Yes, I'm.~~

Part 2: Negative
▶ 01.08

	Negative (−)
I	*I'm not from Italy.*
you	*You're not a teacher.*
we	*We're not from the U.S.*
you	*You're not teachers.*

> 💭 **Tip**
> I am not → I'm not
> You are not → You're not /
>   You aren't
> We are not → We're not /
>   We aren't

I'm not from Brazil. NOT ~~I amn't from Brazil.~~

1B *be*: *he / she / they*

Part 1: Affirmative
▶ 01.16

	+
he	*He's Japanese.*
she	*She's Mexican.*
they	*They're American.*

> 💭 **Tip**
> He is → He's
> She is → She's
> They are → They're

He's Japanese.

She's Mexican.

They're American.

Part 2: Negative and questions
▶ 01.18

	−
he	*He's not Japanese.*
she	*She's not Mexican.*
they	*They're not American.*

> 💭 **Tip**
> He is not → He's not / He isn't
> She is not → She's not /
>   She isn't
> They are not → They're not /
>   They aren't

▶ 01.19

Yes/No questions (?)		Short answers	
he	**Is** he Japanese?	Yes, he **is**.	No, he**'s not**.
she	**Is** she Mexican?	Yes, she **is**.	No, she**'s not**.
they	**Are** they American?	Yes, they **are**.	No, they**'re not**.

▶ 01.20

	Wh- questions (?)
he/she	*Where's he/she from?* *Who's he/she?*
they	*Where are they from?* *Who are they?*

Is he Japanese? NOT ~~Is Japanese?~~ OR ~~He is Japanese?~~
Are they American? NOT ~~Are American?~~ OR ~~They are American?~~
Yes, **he is**. NOT ~~Yes, he's.~~

> 💭 **Tip**
> Where **is** he from? → Where**'s** he from?
> Who **is** she? → Who**'s** she?

1A be: I / you / we

Part 1: Affirmative and questions

a Write sentences with *'re* or *'m*.

1 I am from New York.   *I'm from New York.*
2 We are students.
3 You are Roberto.
4 I am fine, thanks.
5 We are from Mexico.

b Put the words in the correct order to make questions.

1 you / are / how ?   *How are you?*
2 are / from / the U.S. / you ?
3 we / in / Ecuador / are ?
4 OK / I / am ?
5 name / your / what's ?

c ⟫ Now go back to p. 8.

Part 2: Negative

a Write one affirmative (+) and one negative (–) sentence for 1–5.

1 We / from Brazil
  We're from Brazil. We're not from Brazil.
2 You / Rebecca
3 I / a teacher
4 We / in Paris
5 I / OK

b Write short answers.

1 **A** Are you from the U.S.?   3 **A** Are we in Spain?
  B No, ____I'm not____.   **B** No, _____.
2 **A** Are you Eric?   4 **A** Are you students?
  B Yes, _____.   **B** Yes, _____.

c ⟫ Now go back to p. 9.

1B be: he / she / they

Part 1: Affirmative

a Complete the sentences with *he's*, *she's*, or *they're*.

1 _____ Italian.

2 _____ Chinese.

3 _____ Brazilian.

4 _____ Mexican.

5 _____ Spanish.

6 _____ British.

b ⟫ Now go back to p. 11.

Part 2: Negative and questions

a Complete the sentences with *'s not* or *'re not*.

1 She _____ Italian. She's Brazilian.
2 They _____ American. They're English.
3 He _____ Chinese. He's American.
4 They _____ Colombian. They're English.
5 He _____ Spanish. He's Italian.
6 She _____ Brazilian. She's Ecuadorian.

b Check (✓) the correct questions. Correct the wrong questions.

1 ☐ He is Colombian?   4 ☐ Are he Italian?
2 ☐ Is she Brazilian?   5 ☐ She is Chinese?
3 ☐ Are English they?   6 ☐ Are they Japanese?

c Complete the conversations with *is*, *'s not*, *'s*, *are*, *'re not*, or *'re*.

A Who is this?
B He ¹_____ my friend Lee.
A ²_____ he Chinese?
B No, he ³_____. He ⁴_____ from the U.S.
A Who are they?
B They ⁵_____ my friends Nick and Anna.
A ⁶_____ they from England?
B No, they ⁷_____. They ⁸_____ Brazilian.

d ⟫ Now go back to p. 11.

2A be: *it's / it's not*; Possessive adjectives

Part 1: *it's / it's not*

it = a place/thing   *they* = 2+ places/things

▶ 02.04

	+	−
it	It**'s** an old hotel.	It**'s not** a new hotel.
they	They**'re** small houses.	They**'re not** big houses.

▶ 02.05

	Yes/No questions	Short answers	
it	**Is** it a big hotel?	Yes, it **is**.	No, it**'s not**.
they	**Are** they new houses?	Yes, they **are**.	No, they**'re not**.

Is it in Japan? NOT ~~Is in Japan?~~ OR ~~It is in Japan?~~
Yes, **it is**. NOT ~~Yes, it's.~~

Part 2: Possessive adjectives

Pronoun	Possessive adjective	▶ 02.10
I	**my**	**My** apartment is small.
you	**your**	Is this **your** book?
he	**his**	**His** home is old and beautiful.
she	**her**	She's here with **her** friend.
we	**our**	This is **our** home in Quito.
they	**their**	Is that **their** home?

your bag NOT ~~you're bag~~
their house NOT ~~they're house~~

2B Plural nouns

SPELLING: Plural nouns

most words → add *-s*	book → book**s** boy → boy**s** house → house**s**
consonant + *-y* → -y add *-ies*	city → cit**ies** baby → bab**ies**
ends in *-o, -ch, -ss, -s, -sh,* and *-x* → add *-es* Exception: For some *-o* words, add *-s*.	watch → watch**es** glass → glass**es** photo → photo**s**
irregular	knife → kni**ves**

books NOT ~~a books~~

a book   a ticket   an apple

book**s**   two ticket**s**   apple**s**

3A Simple present: *I / you / we / they*

▶ 03.09

	+		−	
I	I **like**	fish.	I **don't like**	fish.
you	You **eat**	meat.	You **don't eat**	meat.
we	We **eat**	a lot of vegetables.	We **don't eat**	a lot of vegetables.
they	They **like**	eggs.	They **don't like**	eggs.

I **don't like** fish. NOT ~~I not like fish.~~

▶ 03.10

Yes/No questions	Short answers	
Do I **like** fish?	Yes, you **do**.	No, you **don't**.
Do you **eat** meat?	Yes, I **do**.	No, I **don't**.
Do we **eat** a lot of vegetables?	Yes, we **do**.	No, we **don't**.
Do they **like** eggs?	Yes, they **do**.	No, they **don't**.

Do you eat meat? NOT ~~You eat meat?~~
Yes, **I do**. NOT ~~Yes, I like.~~
No, **we don't**. NOT ~~No, we don't like.~~

2A *be*: *it's / it's not*; Possessive adjectives

Part 1: *it's / it's not*

a Complete the sentences with *it's* or *they're*.

1 _____ a beautiful town near Barcelona.
2 São Paulo and Rio de Janeiro are big cities. _____ in Brazil.
3 My apartment is small. _____ in a new part of town.
4 Our homes are old. _____ in a nice part of town.
5 The apartments are in an old part of town. _____ big and beautiful.
6 They're from a small town in China. _____ near Beijing.

b Complete the sentences with *it's not* or *they're not*.

1 The houses are in Montana. _____ in Idaho.
2 "Is this your apartment?" "No, _____."
3 Mumbai is a big city. _____ small.
4 They are from Costa Rica. _____ a big country.
5 They are from Ottawa. _____ from Vancouver.
6 Their apartments are very old. _____ in a new part of town.

c ⟫ Now go back to p. 16.

Part 2: Possessive adjectives

a Complete the sentences.

1 "Hi, I'm Jack. What's _____ name?" "I'm Selim."
2 She's from Brazil and _____ name's Maria.
3 They're from the U.S., and _____ names are Sam and Erica.
4 We live in Cartagena. _____ apartment is in an old part of town.
5 "Is this _____ book?" "Yes, it is. Thank you."
6 They're from London, but _____ parents are from Mumbai.

b ⟫ Now go back to p. 17.

2B Plural nouns

a Write the plurals.

1 an egg _____
2 a knife _____
3 a girl _____
4 a country _____
5 a town _____
6 a phone _____
7 a house _____
8 a city _____

b Underline the correct words.

1 Bogotá is *big city / a big city*.
2 Villajoyosa is *a town / towns* in Spain.
3 It's *small / a small* house.
4 They're new *apartment / apartments*.
5 Two *bottle / bottles* of water, please.
6 He's a big *baby / babies*.
7 New York and Washington are *cities / citys* in the U.S.
8 Two *tickets / ticketes* to London, please.

c ⟫ Now go back to p. 19.

3A Simple present: *I / you / we / they*

a Complete the sentences with the words in the box.

do (x2)   don't (x3)   eat

1 I like rice, but I _____ like bread.
2 _____ you like fruit?
3 **A** Do they eat meat? **B** Yes, they _____.
4 We _____ fruit every day.
5 I eat rice, but I _____ like it.
6 **A** Do you like fish? **B** No, I _____.

b Look at the information about the Brown family. Write five sentences about them.

meat	✓	
fish	✗	
vegetables	✓	
rice	✓	
bread	✗	

They eat …   They don't eat …

c Write sentences about things you eat and drink.

I eat rice. I eat vegetables every day. I don't like coffee …

d ⟫ Now go back to p. 25.

3B Adverbs of frequency

▶ 03.20

We **always** have breakfast at 7:00.

I **usually** have a sandwich for lunch.

We **sometimes** eat fish for dinner.

I **never** eat cake.
NOT ~~I never don't eat cake.~~

> ◯ Tip
>
> Adverbs of frequency go **before** the verb.
> NOT **~~Always we have~~** ~~breakfast at 7:00.~~ OR **~~We have always~~** ~~breakfast at 7:00.~~
> The adverb of frequency **sometimes** can go **at the beginning of the sentence**, too.
> **We sometimes eat** fish for dinner. OR **Sometimes we eat** fish for dinner.

4A Simple present: *Wh-* questions

When **do** they **go** to school?

▶ 04.05

Wh- questions with *be*	
What**'s** your name?	My name**'s** Lucia.
When **are** you home?	We**'re** home this evening.
Where **are** they from?	They**'re** from Brazil.

NOT ~~What~~ **~~your name is~~**~~?~~ OR ~~Where~~ **~~you are~~** ~~from?~~

> ◯ Tip
>
> *Wh-* word + *is/are* + person (*you, they*, etc.)?

▶ 04.06

Wh- questions with other verbs	
Where **do** you **live**?	I **live** in La Paz.
What **do** you **study**?	We **study** Chinese.
When **do** they **go** to school?	They **go** to school at 8:00.

NOT ~~Where~~ **~~you live~~**~~?~~ OR ~~Where~~ **~~live you~~**~~?~~

> ◯ Tip
>
> *Wh-* word + *do* + person (*you, they*, etc.) + verb?

4B Simple present: *he / she / it* affirmative

▶ 04.14

	+	
he	My brother **works**	in a hotel.
	He **lives**	in a small house.
she	Ingrid **lives**	in Boston.
	She **works**	in an office.
it	My room **has**	a big window.
	It **has**	a big table.

> ◯ Tip
>
> *I/You/We/They* **work** in a hotel.
> *He/She* **works** in a hotel.

SPELLING: verb + -*s*

most verbs → add -*s*	work → work**s** live → live**s**
consonant + -*y* → -*y* add -*ies*	study → stud**ies**
ends in -*o*, -*ch*, -*ss*, -*s*, -*sh* and -*x* → add -*es*	go → go**es** do → do**es** teach → teach**es**
irregular	have → **has**

He **studies** NOT ~~He studys~~
She **has** NOT ~~She haves~~

3B Adverbs of frequency

a Put the words in the correct order to make sentences.

1 sometimes / at 10:00 / have dinner / we
2 I / in the evening / have coffee / never
3 have a sandwich / I / for lunch / usually
4 we / at home / always / have dinner
5 at lunchtime / always / eat fruit / I
6 usually / in a café / I / have lunch

b Look at Monica's schedule. Complete her sentences with adverbs of frequency.

1 "I _____ have coffee in a small café."
2 "I _____ eat breakfast."
3 "My friends and I _____ have lunch at work."
4 "We _____ have dinner at home."

c ⫸ Now go back to p. 27.

Sunday	Monday	Tuesday	Wednesday	Thursday	Friday	Sat
1	2	3	4	5	6	
	8:00 coffee at Café Blanc		**8:00** coffee at Café Blanc			
	12:30 lunch at work	**12:30** lunch at work	**12:30** lunch at work	**12:30** lunch at work	**12:30** lunch at work	
	7:00 dinner with family	**7:00** dinner with family	**7:00** dinner with family	**7:00** dinner with family	**7:00** dinner with family	

4A Simple present: *Wh-* questions

a Complete the questions with *'s*, *are*, or *do*.

1 Where _____ they work?
2 What _____ you eat for breakfast?
3 Where _____ your home?
4 When _____ you in class?
5 Where _____ you study English?
6 Where _____ you from?
7 What time _____ you go to class every day?
8 When _____ he at home?

b Write questions for the sentences. Use the question word in parentheses.

1 I work in Tokyo. (where)
   Where do you work?
2 We go to work at 7:00 in the morning. (when)
3 I eat a sandwich for lunch. (what)
4 We study at a big language school in Quito. (where)
5 I study business at school. (what)
6 I go to my class at 6:00 in the evening. (when)

c ⫸ Now go back to p. 33.

4B Simple present: *he / she / it* affirmative

a <u>Underline</u> the correct words.

1 She always *drink / drinks* tea for breakfast.
2 My son *studies / studys* Spanish in college.
3 He *works / workes* in a supermarket.
4 The car *have / has* new lights.
5 She has breakfast and then she *gos / goes* to school.
6 The dog *play / plays* in the backyard.

b Look at the picture. Complete the sentences about Carmen with the verbs in the box.

have	drink	eat	live	study

1 She _____ in Madrid.
2 She _____ English.
3 She _____ bananas.
4 She _____ coffee.
5 She _____ a computer.

c ⫸ Now go back to p. 35.

5A *there is / there are*: affirmative

On Regent Street, …
… **there's** a movie theater.
… **there are** two cafés.
… **there are** a lot of people.

There's = There is
There's *a café.* NOT ~~*There a café.*~~
There are *three cafés.*
NOT ~~*There's three cafés.*~~

▶ 05.02

	+	
Singular	***There's***	*a café.* *one café.*
Plural	***There are***	*cafés.* *three cafés.*

5B *there is / there are*: negative and questions

▶ 05.16

	−		−	
Singular	***There isn't***	*a shower.* *a blanket.*	***There's no***	*shower.* *blanket.*
Plural	***There aren't***	*any pillows.* *any rooms.*	***There are no***	*pillows.* *rooms.*

NOT ~~*There's isn't shower.*~~ OR ~~*There's no a shower.*~~
NOT ~~*There are no any pillows.*~~

> 💡 **Tip**
>
> There **is not** a hotel. → There **isn't** a hotel. → There**'s no** hotel.
> There **are not** any cafés. → There **aren't** any cafés. → There **are no** cafés.
> Use *any* after *there are not* and *there aren't.*

▶ 05.17

	Yes/No questions		Short answers	
Singular	***Is there***	*a café?*	*Yes,* **there is**.	*No,* **there isn't**.
Plural	***Are there***	*any small rooms?*	*Yes,* **there are**.	*No,* **there aren't**.

NOT ~~*There is a café?*~~ OR ~~*There are small rooms?*~~
NOT ~~*Yes, there's.*~~ OR ~~*No, there not.*~~

> 💡 **Tip**
>
> Use *any* after *Are there … ?*

Are there any hotels near here?

5A *there is / there are*: affirmative

a Write three more sentences about Regent Street on page 122. Use *there's* or *there are* and the words in the box.

> apartment   car   supermarket

1 _____
2 _____
3 _____

b Look at the picture. Change the sentences to make them true.

1 There's a taxi.
2 There are two restaurants.
3 There's one store.
4 There are three women.
5 There are three girls.
6 There's a boy.
7 There are two schools.

c ⟫ Now go back to p. 40.

5B *there is / there are*: negative and questions

a Complete the sentences with a negative (–) or question (?) form of *there is* or *there are*.

1 _____ any cafés on my street.
2 _____ a movie theater in this part of town.
3 _____ a hotel near the subway station?
4 _____ any stores near the hotel?
5 _____ any restaurants on High Street.
6 _____ a café near here?
7 _____ a restaurant near the movie theater.
8 _____ any supermarkets near the hostel?

b Add *any* to the sentences if possible.

1 There aren't good restaurants in this town.
2 Are there stores near the hotel?
3 Is there a TV in the room?
4 Sorry, there aren't available rooms.
5 There's a café on the first floor.
6 There are two movie theaters near here.

c Complete the conversation with the correct form of *there is / there are*.

A Excuse me, _____ _____ any hotels near here?
B No, _____ _____. But _____ one near the train station.
A And _____ _____ a restaurant near the hotel?
B Yes, _____ _____. It's a very good one.

d Rewrite the sentences using *there's no* or *there are no*.

1 There isn't a TV in the room. *There's no TV in the room.*
2 There aren't hotels on this street. _____
3 There aren't any pillows in the room. _____
4 There isn't a swimming pool. _____
5 There isn't a school in the town. _____
6 There aren't gas stations on this road. _____

e ⟫ Now go back to p. 43.

6A Simple present: *he / she / it* negative

 06.05

	–	
he	He **doesn't work**	on Monday.
she	She **doesn't study**	Spanish.
it	The town **doesn't have**	a bank.

He **doesn't work** on Monday. NOT ~~He doesn't works on Monday.~~
OR ~~He **don't works** on Monday.~~
OR ~~He **not works** on Monday.~~

> 💡 Tip
> I **do not work** at night. → I **don't work** at night.
> He **does not work** at night. → He **doesn't work** at night.

6B Simple present: *he / she / it* questions

 06.13

	Yes/No questions		Short answers	
he	**Does** he	**work** at a bank?	Yes, he **does**.	No, he **doesn't**.
she	**Does** she	**get up** early?	Yes, she **does**.	No, she **doesn't**.
it	**Does** the party	**start** at 9:00?	Yes, it **does**.	No, it **doesn't**.

Does he work in a bank?   NOT ~~Does he works … ?~~
Yes, **she does**.   NOT ~~Yes, she **works**.~~
No, **she doesn't**.   NOT ~~No, she **doesn't work**.~~

 06.14

	Wh- questions		
he	Where	**does** he	**work**?
she	When	**does** she	**get up**?
it	What time	**does** it	**start**?

Where **does she** work?   NOT ~~Where **she does** work?~~
       OR ~~Where **she works**?~~

Does she get up early?

6A Simple present: *he / she / it* negative

a Complete the sentences with *don't* or *doesn't*.

1 They ___don't___ speak French.
2 He _____ like chocolate cake.
3 She _____ eat eggs for breakfast.
4 We _____ go to work early.
5 Eva and Ben _____ like their jobs.
6 Penelope and her sister _____ live in Spain.
7 Her brother _____ work in a bank.
8 My sister, Lucia, and I _____ eat fish.

b Make the sentences negative.

1 Pia works in a store.   *Pia doesn't work in a store.*
2 My brother works in a car factory.
3 My parents like coffee.
4 We live near the subway station.
5 He studies Italian.
6 They go to work early.
7 Akira lives in Tokyo.
8 Their son works in a bank.

c ≫ Now go back to p. 49.

6B Simple present: *he / she / it* questions

a Complete the questions.

1 **A** He works in a restaurant.
  B _____ he like it?
2 **A** I'm a taxi driver.
  B _____ you meet interesting people?
3 **A** My brother's in London.
  B _____ he live there?
4 **A** My children go to school at 7:30.
  B What time _____ they get up?
5 **A** She often works in the evenings.
  B When _____ she get home?

b Underline the correct words.

1 **A** Does your daughter like school?
  B Yes, she *likes* / *does*. She thinks it's great.
2 **A** Do you like ice cream?
  B *Yes* / *No*, I don't. I never eat it.
3 **A** Does he watch baseball?
  B No, he *don't* / *doesn't*. He only likes tennis.
4 **A** Do you start work early?
  B Yes, we *are* / *do*. We start at 5:00 in the morning!
5 **A** Does your wife work in a restaurant?
  B No, she *doesn't work* / *doesn't*. She's a hotel receptionist.

c ≫ Now go back to p. 51.

VOCABULARY FOCUS

1A Countries

a ▶️ 01.11 Listen and write the countries on the map.

---
the U.S.   Brazil   the U.K. / Britain
Ecuador   Spain   Mexico   Colombia
China   Japan

> 🔎 **Tip**
> the U.S. = the United States of America
> the U.K. = the United Kingdom

b ▶️ 01.11 Listen again and practice saying the countries.

c 💬 Add the name of your country in English to the list in a. Practice saying it.

d ≫ Now go back to p. 9.

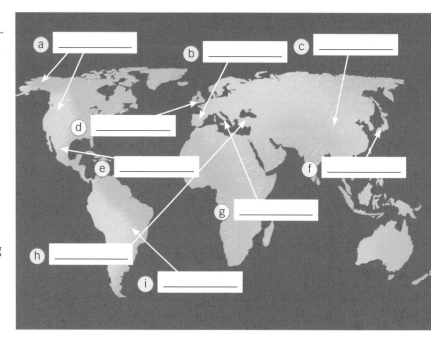

a _____
b _____
c _____
d _____
e _____
f _____
g _____
h _____
i _____

1B Nationalities

a Complete the charts with countries from page 9.

Country	Nationality
	-ian
Australia	Australian
1_____	Brazilian
Canada	Canadian
2_____	Colombian
Ecuador	Ecuadorian
Italy	Italian

Country	Nationality
	-an
3_____	Mexican
4_____	American
	-ish
5_____	Spanish
6_____ / Britain	British
	-ese
7_____	Chinese
8_____	Japanese

b ▶️ 01.14 Listen and repeat the countries and nationalities.

c Write your nationality.
I'm _____.

d 💬 Work in pairs.
Student A: Say a country.
Student B: Say the nationality.

Canada
Canadian

Then switch roles.

e ≫ Now go back to p. 10.

2A Common adjectives

a ▶02.09 Listen and repeat the adjectives.

1 small   big   2 old   new

3 good   bad   4 happy   sad

5 interesting boring   6 easy   difficult

7 right   wrong   8 beautiful   9 funny

b 💬 Work in pairs.

Student A: Say an adjective.
Student B: Say the opposite.

happy   sad

c Complete the sentences with an adjective. There is no correct answer.

1 New York is a _____ city.
2 Harry Potter books are _____.
3 My house is very _____.
4 The English language is _____ for me.
5 My best friend is _____.

💬 Tell a partner your sentences. Are the adjectives the same?

d ≫ Now go back to p. 17.

2B Common objects 1

a book (books)

a bottle of water (bottles of water)

a computer (computers)

a key (keys)

a newspaper (newspapers)

a knife (knives)

a phone (phones)

a ticket (tickets)

a watch (watches)

an umbrella (umbrellas)

a ▶ 02.12 Listen and repeat the objects.

b Write three objects on three pieces of paper. Don't show your partner!

a phone   an umbrella   a book

c 💬 Guess your partner's words.

Is it a watch?   Is it a book?

No.   Yes.

d ≫ Now go back to p. 18.

5B Hotels

a ▶ 05.11 Listen and repeat the words.

bathtub

room

bed

pillow

shower

Wi-Fi

blanket

parking

TV

towel

There's parking at the hotel. NOT ~~There's a parking at the hotel.~~ OR ~~There are parking at the hotel.~~

There's Wi-Fi in the room. NOT ~~There's a Wi-Fi in the room.~~ OR ~~There are Wi-Fi in the room.~~

b 💬 Which word is different in each group? Compare your answers with your partner.

1 shower	pillow	bathtub	4 parking	towel	blanket
2 TV	Wi-Fi	room	5 bed	room	bathtub
3 shower	blanket	pillow			

c ≫ Now go back to p. 42.

3A Food 1

a ▶ 03.04 Listen and repeat the words.

fruit   vegetables   meat   fish

eggs   bread   rice

b 💬 Talk to a partner. What food is in the pictures?

c Match pictures 1–6 with the words in the box.

coffee   soda   juice   milk   tea   water

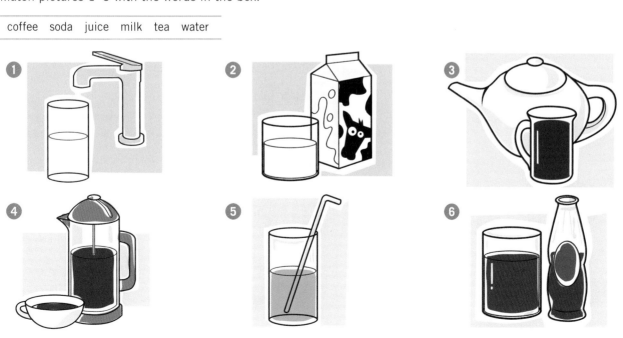

d ▶ 03.05 Listen and check your answers in c. Practice saying the words.

e 💬 Talk to your partner. Which drinks are in the pictures?

I think it's tea.

Maybe it's juice.

f ≫ Now go back to p. 24.

3B Food 2

a ▶03.11 Listen and repeat the words.

breakfast   lunch   dinner

I have breakfast at 7:30. NOT ~~I have a breakfast at 7:30.~~
She has lunch at 12:30. NOT ~~She has a lunch at 12:30.~~
We have dinner at 7:00. NOT ~~We have a dinner at 7.00.~~

b ▶03.12 Match the words in the box with pictures 1–12. Listen and check your answers.
Then listen and repeat.

orange   sandwich   butter   cookie   banana   pizza   potato   tomato   apple   ice cream   cheese   cake

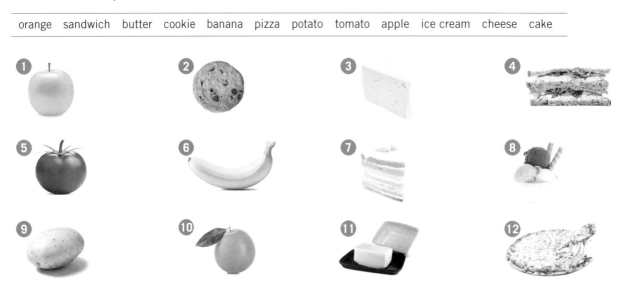

c 💬 Which food in b do you eat for … ?

• breakfast • lunch • dinner

d ≫ Now go back to p. 27.

2B Numbers 1

a ▶ 02.19 Listen and repeat the numbers.

1	**2**	**3**	**4**	**5**	**6**	**7**	**8**	**9**	**10**
one	two	three	four	five	six	seven	eight	nine	ten

11	**12**	**13**	**14**	**15**	**16**	**17**	**18**	**19**
eleven	twelve	thirteen	fourteen	fifteen	sixteen	seventeen	eighteen	nineteen

thirteen NOT ~~threeteen~~, *fifteen* NOT ~~fiveteen~~

20	**30**	**40**	**50**	**60**	**70**	**80**	**90**
twenty	thirty	forty	fifty	sixty	seventy	eighty	ninety

thirty NOT ~~threety~~, *forty* NOT ~~fourty~~, *fifty* NOT ~~fivety~~

b ▶ 02.20 Listen to a–g. <u>Underline</u> the number you hear.

a 13 / 30   c 15 / 50   e 17 / 70   g 19 / 90
b 14 / 40   d 16 / 60   f 18 / 80

c ≫ Now go back to p. 19.

3B Time

a ▶ 03.15 Match the clocks with the times in the box. Listen and check.

two o'clock   twenty after two   (a) quarter after two
two thirty   (a) quarter to two   twenty to two

b ▶ 03.15 Listen again and repeat the times.

c Complete the sentences.

1 My English class is at _____.
2 My favorite TV show is at _____.
3 My school / job starts at _____.

💬🗩 Tell a partner your sentences.

d ≫ Now go back to p. 27.

4B Numbers 2

a ▶ 04.13 Listen and repeat the numbers.

21	**34**	**42**	**57**	**63**	**79**	**85**	**99**	**100**
twenty-one	thirty-four	forty-two	fifty-seven	sixty-three	seventy-nine	eighty-five	ninety-nine	a/one hundred

thirty-four NOT ~~thirty and four~~ OR ~~four and thirty~~

b 💬🗩 Work with a partner.

Student A: Say a number in the box.
Student B: Say the next two numbers.

52   41   29   68   98   36   82   75   59

fifty-two

fifty-three, fifty-four

c ≫ Now go back to p. 35.

a ▶ **04.02** Listen to the sentences. Repeat the verbs.

1 We **live** in a big house.

2 I **work** in a factory.

¡Hola!

3 I **speak** Spanish.

4 We **study** at school.

5 I **go** to the movies every weekend.

6 I **teach** young children.

7 We **play** tennis on Saturdays.

8 I **meet** my friends for coffee every day.

b Complete the phrases with verbs in a.

1 ____work____ in an office / in a bank
2 _____ soccer / the guitar
3 _____ in an apartment / in New York
4 _____, 5 _____ and 6 _____ Italian
7 _____ in college
8 _____ people / a friend
9 _____ to the gym / home

c Write two sentences about you with phrases in a and b.

I study English. I play soccer.

💬 Tell a partner your sentences.

d ≫ Now go back to p. 32.

4B Family and people

a ▶ 04.09 Listen and repeat the words.

b Look at the words in a. Complete 1–10.

1 _____
2 _____
3 _____
4 _____
5 _____
6 _____
7 _____
8 _____
9 _____
10 _____

c ▶ 04.10 Listen and repeat the words.

d Complete the sentences with words from a and c.

1 They have three c_____n, a b_____y and two g_____s.
2 I'm Olivia and this is David. He's my h_____d.
3 That w_____n is my s_____r.
4 They have a new b_____y. It's a g_____l. Her name's Lucia.
5 My yoga class has ten p_____e: nine w_____n and only one m_____n!

e ≫ Now go back to p. 34.

a ▶ 05.04 Listen and repeat the places.

subway station

supermarket

school

hotel

hospital

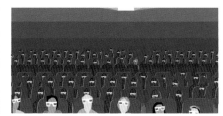
movie theater

restaurant

bank

store

café

swimming pool

park

museum

beach

bus stop

b 💬 Talk to your partner. Where are these signs?

I think 1 is at a swimming pool, or maybe a beach.

❶

❷

❸

❹

❺

❻

❼

❽

c ≫ Now go back to p. 41.

6A Jobs

a ▶ **06.03** Listen and repeat the jobs.

soccer player

student

receptionist

server

taxi driver

factory worker

bank teller

sales assistant

businessman / businesswoman

chef

office worker

IT worker

teacher

doctor

b Cover the words and pictures in a. Correct the spelling in each job. Then check your answers.

1 studint
2 servar
3 factery worker
4 sales asistant
5 taxi drivar
6 socer player
7 receptonist
8 bank tellr
9 ofice worker

c 💬 Do you know people who do the jobs in a? Tell your partner.

My father is a taxi driver.

My friend Kumiko is a chef.

d ≫ Now go back to p. 49.

a ▶ 06.08 Listen to Danny's daily routine and complete the times.

1 Danny **wakes up** at
_____.

2 He **gets up** at
_____.

3 He **has breakfast** at
_____.

4 He **goes to work** at
_____.

5 He **starts work** at
_____.

6 He **has lunch** at
_____.

7 He **finishes work** at
_____.

8 He **gets home** at
_____.

9 He **has dinner** at
_____.

10 He **goes to bed** at
_____.

b ▶ 06.09 Listen and repeat the verb phrases.

wake get	up	have	breakfast lunch dinner coffee	go	to school to work to bed	start finish	work	get arrive	home	take	a shower

have breakfast/lunch/dinner NOT ~~have the breakfast, have a lunch~~
go to work NOT ~~go to the work~~
go to bed NOT ~~go in the bed~~

c Read about Pablo's daily routine. Then complete the sentences about him with words in a and b.

I sleep from 11:00 to 7:00 every night.
In the morning, I get up and have breakfast. I finish at 7:30.
It's 30 minutes by bus to go to work.
I work from 8:30 until 12:30, then I have lunch for half an hour.
Then I work for three hours until I go home.

1 He _____ at 7:00.
2 He _____ at 7:30.
3 He _____ at 8:00.
4 He _____ at 8:30.
5 He _____ at 12:30.
6 He _____ at 4:00.
7 He _____ at 11:00 at night.

d ≫ Now go back to p. 50.

This page is intentionally left blank.

WRITING PLUS

1C Capital letters and periods

a Look at the sentence. Read the information about capital letters and periods.

My name's Sophia Taylor.

Capital letters
We use capital letters (*A, B, C, D* …):
- for names (***S**ophia **T**aylor, **B**en **W**ilson, **M**aria **G**onzález*)
- names of places (***T**oronto, **C**anada, **H**igh **S**treet*)
- for nationalities (***I**talian, **B**ritish, **C**hinese*)
- at the beginning of a sentence (***M**y name's* …)

Periods
. = period
We usually use periods at the end of sentences.

My name's Sophia Taylor.

b Write the capital letters.

1 a	A	4 e		7 q	
2 b		5 g		8 r	
3 d		6 h		9 t	

c Add capital letters and periods to each sentence.

> they're married.
1 we're from brazil
2 he's a student
3 this is ruben
4 i'm in a class with amy lee
5 my name is sandro
6 their apartment is in mexico city it's small

d ≫ Now go back to p. 13.

2C The alphabet and spelling

Part 1: The alphabet

a ▶02.26 Listen to how we say the letters of the alphabet.

/eɪ/ (*day*)	/i/ (*we*)	/e/ (*ten*)	/aɪ/ (*hi*)	/oʊ/ (*no*)	/u/ (*you*)	/ɑ/ (*car*)
Aa	Bb	Ff	Ii	Oo	Qq	Rr
Hh	Cc	Ll	Yy		Uu	
Jj	Dd	Mm			Ww	
Kk	Ee	Nn			("double u")	
	Gg	Ss				
	Pp	Xx				
	Tt					
	Vv					
	Zz					

b Add the letters to the group with similar sounds. Say the letters.

R   H   Q   O   Z   Y   C   F

1 (y**ou**) U, Q, W
2 (d**ay**) J, __, A, K
3 (h**i**) I, __
4 (w**e**) T, __, B, D, E, G, P, V, __
5 (t**en**) N, L, __, M, S, X
6 (c**ar**) __
7 (n**o**) __

c ≫ Now go back to p. 20.

Part 2: Spelling

Some words in English have double letters in their written form.
*umbre**ll**a*
Other words in English have letters in their written form that might seem different from what you hear.
***c**ity*

d ▶02.30 Correct the spelling. Listen and check. Then practice spelling the words.

1 adress	5 smal	9 rong
2 bok	6 dificult	10 nife
3 umbrela	7 intresting	
4 hapy	8 rite	

e ≫ Now go back to p. 21.

3C Contractions

a Look at the sentences and read about contractions.

I'm at a café with Hannah. **She's** my friend from work.

I'm (contraction) = *I am* *She's* (contraction) = *She is*
We use contractions in speaking and writing, usually in informal situations.

be: affirmative and negative

+		–	
Full form	**Contraction**	**Full form**	**Contraction**
I am	*I'm*	*I am not*	*I'm not*
you are	*you're*	*you are not*	*you're not / you aren't*
we are	*we're*	*we are not*	*we're not / we aren't*
he is	*he's*	*he is not*	*he's not / he isn't*
she is	*she's*	*she is not*	*she's not / she isn't*
it is	*it's*	*it is not*	*it's not / it isn't*
they are	*they're*	*they are not*	*they're not / they aren't*

It is a pizza. → **It's** a pizza.

Simple present: negative

Full form	**Contraction**
I/you/we do not	*I/you/we don't*

I do not eat fish. → *I don't eat fish.*

b Match the contractions in the box with 1–8.

> we're not   it's not   don't   I'm   you're   she's
> they're   we're

1 you are _____
2 she is _____
3 I am _____
4 do not _____
5 they are _____
6 we are not _____
7 we are _____
8 it is not _____

c Add the words in parentheses to each sentence. Use contractions.

1 _____ from Sweden. (He is)
2 _____ tomatoes. (They are)
3 _____ five o'clock. (It is not)
4 I _____ have a big meal in the evening. (do not)
5 _____ a teacher. (You are not)
6 _____ OK. (I am)
7 We _____ eat meat. (do not)
8 _____ Spanish. (I am not)

d ≫ Now go back to p. 29. Try to use contractions in your text message.

4C Word order

a Look at the examples and the word order.

Word order
- **subject + verb**
I work.
You don't work.
- **subject + verb + object**
Emma and Charlotte don't have a brother.
They speak Spanish.
- **subject + verb + preposition + noun**
My daughters are in college.
They don't live in an apartment.
- **subject + verb + object + preposition + noun**
I don't have a phone in my bag.
I like milk in my coffee.

We can use *here* or *there* after a verb.
*I live **there**.*
*You don't work **here**.*

b Check (✓) the correct sentences.

1 a ☐ Tennis we play.
　 b ☐ We play tennis.
2 a ☐ I don't teach children.
　 b ☐ Don't teach children I.
3 a ☐ They there don't study.
　 b ☐ They don't study there.
4 a ☐ My sister in Japan lives.
　 b ☐ My sister lives in Japan.
5 a ☐ These are my friends.
　 b ☐ These my friends are.
6 a ☐ I have an apartment in New York.
　 b ☐ I in New York have an apartment.

c Put the words in the correct order to make sentences. Remember to use capital letters and periods.

1 don't speak / they / German
2 there / have coffee / you
3 we / in a factory / don't work
4 teaches / at the university / my dad / Italian
5 the computer / I / at the office / don't like
6 have / in Canada / a nice house / they

d ≫ Now go back to p. 37.

5C *and* and *but*

a Look at the sentences and read about *and* and *but*.

There's a beautiful park near the hotel, **and** there are stores on the next street.
Our hotel is in a nice part of town, **but** it's really small.

☺	*and*	☺
There's a beautiful park near the hotel,	and	there are stores on the next street.

☹	*and*	☹
The hotel's not very big,	and	it's not near Sebastien's apartment.

☹	*but*	☺
The hotel is really small,	but	it's in in a nice part of town.

☺	*but*	☹
His apartment is nice,	but	it's not near our hotel.

b Underline the correct words.

1 I love New York City, but it's very *expensive / nice*.
2 The hotel has free Wi-Fi, and *there's / it doesn't have* a TV in every room.
3 Libya is a very hot country, but *the old houses are always cool / it's sometimes 55°C*.
4 There are a lot of expensive hotels, but *there are a lot of / there aren't any* cheap hostels.
5 There are a lot of good books in the bookstore, and *they are very boring / the sales assistants are very friendly*.
6 The Maris Hotel is beautiful, and *it's near the ocean / the restaurant isn't very good*.

c Add *and* or *but* to each sentence.

1 I live in Spain, _____ I don't speak Spanish.
2 The food is good, _____ it's very expensive!
3 Their house is nice, _____ it's near the bus station.
4 This hotel room is small, _____ the shower is cold.
5 The city has a good university, _____ I'd like to study there.
6 There isn't a supermarket here, _____ there is a market on the next street.

d ⟫ Now go back to p. 45. Try to use *and* and *but* in your writing.

6C *because* and *also*

a Look at the sentences and read about *because* and *also*.

I walk to work every day **because** my apartment is near the office.
We go out to a café for coffee every day. We **also** have lunch there.

We use *because* and *also* to join ideas.

- *Because* joins two ideas in <u>one</u> sentence. We use *because* to give a reason. It answers the question *Why?*

Why do you like your job?

It's interesting.

  *I like my job **because** it's interesting.*
  *He sleeps in the morning **because** he works at night.*
- *Also* joins two ideas in <u>two</u> sentences. It means *and*.
  He plays baseball and tennis. He plays soccer.
  *He plays baseball and tennis. He **also** plays soccer.*
  (= He plays baseball, tennis, and soccer.)
- We use *also* before the verb:
  *He sleeps in the morning. He **also** sleeps in the afternoon.*
- We use *also* after *be*:
  *I'm a doctor. I'm **also** a teacher.*

b Underline the correct answers.

1 She plays basketball *also she teaches basketball. / . She also teaches basketball.*
2 I feel good in the morning *because I sleep for seven hours at night. / . Because I sleep for seven hours at night.*
3 I speak English. I also speak Italian because my parents *Italian / are Italian*.
4 Michael works at night. His wife *also works / works also* at night.
5 We always eat at home because *like / we like* cooking.
6 He's a student. He *also is / 's also* a waiter.

c Use *because* and *also* to join the ideas.

> I want to go shopping. I need some cups. (because)
  I want to go shopping because I need some cups.
> She teaches English at the school. She teaches Turkish. (also)
  She teaches English at the school. She also teaches Turkish.
1 I don't like my job. It's boring. (because)
2 She doesn't have breakfast. She isn't hungry in the morning. (because)
3 I need to make lunch. I need to go to the supermarket. (also)
4 The children are nice. They're very funny. (also)

d ⟫ Now go back to p. 53. Try to use *because* and *also* in your writing.

This page is intentionally left blank.

Acknowledgments

The authors and publishers acknowledge the following sources of copyright material and are grateful for the permissions granted. While every effort has been made, it has not always been possible to identify the sources of all the material used, or to trace all copyright holders. If any omissions are brought to our notice, we will be happy to include the appropriate acknowledgments on reprinting and in the next update to the digital edition, as applicable.

Key:
U = Unit, CL = Classroom Language, C = Communication Plus, G = Grammar Focus, V = Vocabulary Focus

Photographs
All the photographs are sourced from Getty Images.
Front cover photography by Don Mason/Getty Images.
CL: Alexis84/iStock/Getty Images Plus; Witthaya Prasongsin/Moment; Eric Audras/PhotoAlto; Image Source; Farknot_Architect/iStock/Getty Images Plus; SDI Productions/E+; F. Lukasseck/Radius Images; **U1:** Oliver Burston/Ikon Images/Getty Images Plus; Alex Goodlett/Getty Images Sport; Sean M. Haffey/Getty Images Sport; Clive Brunskill/Getty Images Sport; Chris Brunskill/Fantasista/Getty Images Sport; Lucas Uebel/Getty Images Sport; Jordan Mansfield/Getty Images Sport; Visual China Group; Clasos/LatinContent Editorial; Franckreporter/E+; Phillip Waterman/Cultura; Jacoblund/iStock/Getty Images Plus; **U2:** Jeff Kowalsky/AFP; Janoka82/iStock/Getty Images Plus; Chiyacat/iStock/Getty Images Plus; Karol Kozlowski/robertharding/Getty Images Plus; Charlie Dean/Caiaimage; Fuse/Corbis; Thinkstock/Stockbyte; Tassii/iStock/Getty Images Plus; ER Productions Limited/DigitalVision; Tulcarion/E+; **U3:** Caiaimage; Mphillips007/iStock/Getty Images Plus; AlexPro9500/iStock/Getty Images Plus; Anilakkus/iStock/Getty Images Plus; Baibaz/iStock/Getty Images Plus; pidjoe/iStock/Getty Images Plus; Stockcam/E+; Dszc/iStock/Getty Images Plus; Lane Oatey/Gurpal Singh Datta; Eli_asenova/E+; Vitalina/iStock/Getty Images Plus; JohnGollop/E+; JoeGough/iStock/Getty Images Plus; VvoeVale/iStock/Getty Images Plus; Hispanolistic/E+; Skynesher/E+; Monkeybusinessimages/iStock/Getty Images Plus; XiXinXing; Ridofranz/iStock/Getty Images Plus; Nadofotos/iStock/Getty Images Plus; Vinnstock/iStock/Getty Images Plus; Creacart/iStock/Getty Images Plus; Erstudiostok/iStock/Getty Images Plus; Portra/E+; Bim/E+; **U4:** Michael Cogliantry/Taxi/Getty Images Plus; Compassionate Eye Foundation/Robert Kent/; PeopleImages/E+; Kali9/E+; Efenzi/iStock/Gett; Henryk Sadura/Moment; Sergio Monti/EyeEm; Bojan89iStock/Getty Images Plus; Sambrogio/E+; Albert L. Ortega/Getty Images Entertainment; Mike Coppola/WireImage; Christopher Polk/Getty Images Entertainment; Kevork Djansezian/Getty Images Entertainment; Quality Sport Images/Getty Images Sport; Dimitrios Kambouris/WireImage; Aldomurillo/E+; Westend61; Kathleen Finlay/Cultura; Ariel Skelley/DigitalVision; Morsa Images/E+; **U5:** Pierre Dunnigan/500px; Miroslav_1/iStock Editorial/Getty Images Plus; IPGGutenbergUKLtd/iStock/Getty Images Plus; Andreka/iStock/Getty Images Plus; Monkeybusinessimages/Getty Images Plus; YinYang/E+; JackF/iStock/Getty Images Plus; Hispanolistic/E+; MangoStar_Studio/iStock/Getty Images Plus; Jupiterimages/Goodshoot/Gett; Yogenyogeny/iStock/Getty Images Plus; northlightimages/iStock/Getty Images Plus; Jupiterimages/Stockbyte; Micah Wright/First Light/Getty Images Plus; Kitti Boonnitrod/Moment; Tpopova/iStock/Getty Images Plus; Anadolu Agency; Lorado/E+; Chalffy/iStock; **U6:** Westend61; Hugh Sitton/Corbis/Getty Images Plus; Klaus Vedfelt/DigitalVision; FG Trade/E+; Philipp Nemenz/Cultura; Andresr/E+; Commercial Eye/Stone/Gett; TAGSTOCK1/iStock/Getty Images Plus; DragonImages/iStock/Getty Images Plus; Peopleimages/E+; Skynesher/E+; Jetta Productions Inc/DigitalVision; Rowan Jordan/iStock/Getty Images Plus; Kurt Budiarto Photography/Moment Open; Niqin/E+; Adamkaz/E+; Mediaphotos/iStock/Getty Images Plus; Robert Daly/Caiaimage.

The following images are sourced from other Sourced/libraries.
U3: Danita Delimont/Alamy; **U5:** © Gehry Partners, LLP, © Frank O. Gehry and © Iwan Baan 2014.

Commissioned photography by Gareth Boden:U1; U2

We are grateful to The Stephen Perse 6th Form College, Cambridge, for their help with the commissioned photography.

Illustrations
Illustrations by QBS Learning; Mark Bird; Mark Duffin; Sally Elford; John Goodwin (Eye Candy Illustration); Dusan Lakicevic (Beehive Illustration); Roger Penwill; Gavin Reece (New Division); Martin Sanders (Beehive Illustration); Sean 290 (KJA Artists); David Semple; Marie-Eve Tremblay (Colagene); Andrea Turvey (Eye Candy Illustration); Gary Venn (Lemonade Illustration).

Typeset by QBS Learning.

Audio by John Marshall Media.

Corpus

Development of this publication has made use of the Cambridge English Corpus(CEC). The CEC is a computer database of contemporary spoken and written English, which currently stands at over one billion words. It includes British English, American English and other varieties of English. It also includes the Cambridge Learner Corpus, developed in collaboration with the University of Cambridge ESOL Examinations. Cambridge University Press has built up the CEC to provide evidence about language use that helps us to produce better language teaching materials.

English Profile

This product is informed by English Vocabulary Profile, built as part of English Profile, a collaborative program designed to enhance the learning, teaching and assessment of English worldwide. Its main funding partners are Cambridge University Press and Cambridge Assessment English and its aim is to create a "profile" for English, linked to the Common European Framework of Reference for Languages (CEFR). English Profile outcomes, such as the English Vocabulary Profile, will provide detailed information about the language that learners can be expected to demonstrate at each CEFR level, offering a clear benchmark for learners' proficiency. For more information, please visit www.englishprofile.org.

CALD

The Cambridge Advanced Learner's Dictionary is the world's most widely used dictionary for learners of English. Including all the words and phrases that learners are likely to come across, it also has easy-to-understand definitions and example sentences to show how the word is used in context. The Cambridge Advanced Learner's Dictionary is available online at dictionary.cambridge.org.

Shaftesbury Road, Cambridge CB2 8EA, United Kingdom

One Liberty Plaza, 20th Floor, New York, NY 10006, USA

477 Williamstown Road, Port Melbourne, VIC 3207, Australia

314–321, 3rd Floor, Plot 3, Splendor Forum, Jasola District Centre, New Delhi – 110025, India

103 Penang Road, #05–06/07, Visioncrest Commercial, Singapore 238467

Cambridge University Press & Assessment is a department of the University of Cambridge.

We share the University's mission to contribute to society through the pursuit of education, learning and research at the highest international levels of excellence.

www.cambridge.org
Information on this title: www.cambridge.org/9781108862271

© Cambridge University Press & Assessment 2022

First published 2022

20 19 18 17 16 15 14 13 12 11 10 9 8 7 6 5

Printed in Poland by Opolgraf

A catalogue record for this publication is available from the British Library

ISBN 978-1-108-81813-1 Starter Student's Book with eBook
ISBN 978-1-108-81831-5 Starter Student's Book A with eBook
ISBN 978-1-108-81832-2 Starter Student's Book B with eBook
ISBN 978-1-108-86221-9 Starter Student's Book with Digital Pack
ISBN 978-1-108-86227-1 Starter Student's Book A with Digital Pack
ISBN 978-1-108-86229-5 Starter Student's Book B with Digital Pack
ISBN 978-1-108-81814-8 Starter Workbook with Answers
ISBN 978-1-108-81815-5 Starter Workbook A with Answers
ISBN 978-1-108-81819-3 Starter Workbook B with Answers
ISBN 978-1-108-81820-9 Starter Workbook without Answers
ISBN 978-1-108-81825-4 Starter Workbook A without Answers
ISBN 978-1-108-81826-1 Starter Workbook B without Answers
ISBN 978-1-108-81827-8 Starter Full Contact with eBook
ISBN 978-1-108-81828-5 Starter Full Contact A with eBook
ISBN 978-1-108-81829-2 Starter Full Contact B with eBook
ISBN 978-1-108-86223-3 Starter Full Contact with Digital Pack
ISBN 978-1-108-86224-0 Starter Full Contact A with Digital Pack
ISBN 978-1-108-86225-7 Starter Full Contact B with Digital Pack
ISBN 978-1-108-81833-9 Starter Teacher's Book with Digital Pack
ISBN 978-1-108-81810-0 Starter Presentation Plus

Additional resources for this publication at www.cambridge.org/americanempower